OBJECT MATCHING IN DIGITAL VIDEO USING DESCRIPTORS WITH PYTHON AND TKINTER

VIVIAN SIAHAAN
RISMON HASIHOLAN SIANIPAR

Copyright © 2024 BALIGE Publishing

All rights reserved. No part of this book may be reproduced, stored in a retrieval system, or transmitted in any form or by any means, without the prior written permission of the publisher, except in the case of brief quotations embedded in critical articles or reviews. Every effort has been made in the preparation of this book to ensure the accuracy of the information presented. However, the information contained in this book is sold without warranty, either express or implied. Neither the authors, nor BALIGE Publishing or its dealers and distributors, will be held liable for any damages caused or alleged to have been caused directly or indirectly by this book. BALIGE Publishing has endeavored to provide trademark information about all of the companies and products mentioned in this book by the appropriate use of capitals. However, BALIGE Publishing cannot guarantee the accuracy of this information.

Published: JUNE 2024
Production reference: 0200624
Published by BALIGE Publishing Ltd.
BALIGE, North Sumatera

ABOUT THE AUTHOR

Vivian Siahaan is a highly motivated individual with a passion for continuous learning and exploring new areas. Born and raised in Hinalang Bagasan, Balige, situated on the picturesque banks of Lake Toba, she completed her high school education at SMAN 1 Balige. Vivian's journey into the world of programming began with a deep dive into various languages such as Java, Android, JavaScript, CSS, C++, Python, R, Visual Basic, Visual C#, MATLAB, Mathematica, PHP, JSP, MySQL, SQL Server, Oracle, Access, and more. Starting from scratch, Vivian diligently studied programming, focusing on mastering the fundamental syntax and logic. She honed her skills by creating practical GUI applications, gradually building her expertise. One particular area of interest for Vivian is animation and game development, where she aspires to make significant contributions. Alongside her programming and mathematical pursuits, she also finds joy in indulging in novels, nurturing her love for literature. Vivian Siahaan's passion for programming and her extensive knowledge are reflected in the numerous ebooks she has authored. Her works, published by Sparta Publisher, cover a wide range of topics, including "Data Structure with Java," "Java Programming: Cookbook," "C++ Programming: Cookbook," "C Programming For High Schools/Vocational Schools and Students," "Java Programming for SMA/SMK," "Java Tutorial: GUI, Graphics and Animation," "Visual Basic Programming: From A to Z," "Java Programming for Animation and Games," "C# Programming for SMA/SMK and Students," "MATLAB For Students and Researchers," "Graphics in JavaScript: Quick Learning Series," "JavaScript Image Processing Methods: From A to Z," "Java GUI Case Study: AWT & Swing," "Basic CSS and JavaScript," "PHP/MySQL Programming: Cookbook," "Visual Basic: Cookbook," "C++ Programming for High Schools/Vocational Schools and Students," "Concepts and Practices of C++," "PHP/MySQL For Students," "C# Programming: From A to Z," "Visual Basic for SMA/SMK and Students," and "C# .NET and SQL Server for High School/Vocational School and Students." Furthermore, at the ANDI Yogyakarta publisher, Vivian Siahaan has contributed to several notable books, including "Python Programming Theory and Practice," "Python GUI Programming," "Python GUI and Database," "Build From Zero School Database Management System In Python/MySQL," "Database Management System in Python/MySQL," "Python/MySQL For Management Systems of Criminal Track Record Database," "Java/MySQL For Management Systems of Criminal Track Records Database," "Database and Cryptography Using Java/MySQL," and "Build From Zero School Database Management System With Java/MySQL." Vivian's diverse range of expertise in programming languages, combined with her passion for exploring new horizons, makes her a dynamic and versatile individual in the field of technology. Her dedication to learning, coupled with her strong analytical and problem-solving skills, positions her as a valuable asset in any programming endeavor. Vivian Siahaan's contributions to the world of programming and literature continue to inspire and empower aspiring programmers and readers alike.

Rismon Hasiholan Sianipar, born in Pematang Siantar in 1994, is a distinguished researcher and expert in the field of electrical engineering. After completing his education at SMAN 3 Pematang Siantar, Rismon ventured to the city of Jogjakarta to pursue his academic journey. He obtained his Bachelor of Engineering (S.T) and Master of Engineering (M.T) degrees in Electrical Engineering from Gadjah Mada University in 1998 and 2001, respectively, under the guidance of esteemed professors, Dr. Adhi Soesanto and Dr. Thomas Sri Widodo. During his studies, Rismon focused on researching non-stationary signals and their energy analysis using time-frequency maps. He explored the dynamic nature of signal energy distribution on time-frequency maps and developed innovative techniques using discrete wavelet transformations to design non-linear filters for data pattern analysis. His research showcased the application of these techniques in various fields. In recognition of his academic prowess, Rismon was awarded the prestigious Monbukagakusho scholarship by the Japanese Government in 2003. He went on to pursue his Master of Engineering (M.Eng) and Doctor of Engineering (Dr.Eng) degrees at Yamaguchi University, supervised by Prof. Dr. Hidetoshi Miike. Rismon's master's and doctoral theses revolved around combining the SR-FHN (Stochastic Resonance Fitzhugh-Nagumo) filter strength with the cryptosystem ECC (elliptic curve cryptography) 4096-bit. This innovative approach effectively suppressed noise in digital images and videos while ensuring their authenticity. Rismon's research findings have been published in renowned international scientific journals, and his patents have been officially registered in Japan. Notably, one of his patents, with registration number 2008-009549, gained recognition. He actively collaborates with several universities and research institutions in Japan, specializing in cryptography, cryptanalysis, and digital forensics, particularly in the areas of audio, image, and video analysis. With a passion for knowledge sharing, Rismon has authored numerous national and international scientific articles and authored several national books. He has also actively participated in workshops related to cryptography, cryptanalysis, digital watermarking, and digital forensics. During these workshops, Rismon has assisted Prof. Hidetoshi Miike in developing applications related to digital image and video processing, steganography, cryptography, watermarking, and more, which serve as valuable training materials. Rismon's field of interest encompasses multimedia security, signal processing, digital image and video analysis, cryptography, digital communication, digital forensics, and data compression. He continues to advance his research by developing applications using programming languages such as Python, MATLAB, C++, C, VB.NET, C#.NET, R, and Java. These applications serve both research and commercial purposes, further contributing to the advancement of signal and image analysis. Rismon Hasiholan Sianipar is a dedicated researcher and expert in the field of electrical engineering, particularly in the areas of signal processing, cryptography, and digital forensics. His academic achievements, patented inventions, and extensive publications demonstrate his commitment to advancing knowledge in these fields. Rismon's contributions to academia and his collaborations with prestigious institutions in Japan have solidified his position as a respected figure in the scientific community. Through his ongoing research and development of innovative applications, Rismon continues to make significant contributions to the field of electrical engineering.

ABOUT THE BOOK

The first project is a sophisticated tool for comparing and matching visual features between images using the Scale-Invariant Feature Transform (SIFT) algorithm. Built with Tkinter, it features an intuitive GUI enabling users to load images, adjust SIFT parameters (e.g., number of features, thresholds), and customize BFMatcher settings. The tool detects keypoints invariant to scale, rotation, and illumination, computes descriptors, and uses BFMatcher for matching. It includes a ratio test for match reliability and visualizes matches with customizable lines. Designed for accessibility and efficiency, SIFTMacher_NEW.py integrates advanced computer vision techniques to support diverse applications in image processing, research, and industry.

The second project is a Python-based GUI application designed for image matching using the ORB (Oriented FAST and Rotated BRIEF) algorithm, leveraging OpenCV for image processing, Tkinter for GUI development, and PIL for image format handling. Users can load and match two images, adjusting parameters such as number of features, scale factor, and edge threshold directly through sliders and options provided in the interface. The application computes keypoints and descriptors using ORB, matches them using a BFMatcher based on Hamming distance, and visualizes the top matches by drawing lines between corresponding keypoints on a combined image. ORBMacher.py offers a user-friendly platform for experimenting with ORB's capabilities in feature detection and image matching, suitable for educational and practical applications in computer vision and image processing.

The third project is a Python application designed for visualizing keypoint matches between images using the FAST (Features from Accelerated Segment Test) detector and SIFT (Scale-Invariant Feature Transform) descriptor. Built with Tkinter for the GUI, it allows users to load two images, adjust detector parameters like threshold and non-maximum suppression, and visualize matches in real-time. The interface includes controls for image loading, parameter adjustment, and features a scrollable canvas for exploring matched results. The core functionality employs OpenCV for image processing tasks such as keypoint detection, descriptor computation, and matching using a Brute Force Matcher with L2 norm. This tool is aimed at enhancing user interaction and analysis in computer vision applications.

The fourth project creates a GUI for matching keypoints between images using the AGAST (Adaptive and Generic Accelerated Segment Test) algorithm with BRIEF descriptors. Utilizing OpenCV for image processing and Tkinter for the interface, it initializes a window titled "AGAST Image Matcher" with a control_frame for buttons and sliders. Users can load two images using load_button1 and load_button2, which trigger file dialogs and display images on a scrollable canvas via load_image1(), load_image2(), and show_image(). Adjustable parameters include AGAST threshold and BRIEF descriptor bytes. Clicking match_button invokes match_images(), checking image loading, detecting keypoints with AGAST, computing BRIEF descriptors, and using BFMatcher for matching and visualization. The matched image, enhanced with color-coded lines, replaces previous images on the canvas, ensuring clear, interactive results presentation.

The fifth project is a Python-based application that utilizes the AKAZE feature detection algorithm from OpenCV for matching keypoints between images. Implemented with Tkinter for the GUI, it features a "AKAZE Image Matcher" window with buttons for loading images and adjusting AKAZE parameters like detection threshold, octaves, and octave layers. Upon loading images via file dialog, the app reads and displays them on a scrollable canvas, ensuring smooth navigation for large images. The match_images method manages keypoint detection using AKAZE and descriptor matching via BFMatcher with Hamming distance, sorting matches for visualization with color-coded lines. It updates the canvas with the matched image, clearing previous content for clarity and enhancing user interaction in image analysis tasks.

The sixth project is a Tkinter-based Python application designed to facilitate the matching and visualization of keypoint descriptors between two images using the BRISK feature detection and description algorithm. Upon initialization, it creates a window titled "BRISK Image Matcher" with a canvas (control_frame) for hosting buttons ("Load Image 1", "Load Image 2", "Match Images") and sliders to adjust BRISK parameters like Threshold, Octaves, and Pattern Scale. Loaded images are displayed on canvas_frame with scrollbars for navigation, utilizing methods like load_image1() and load_image2() to handle image loading and show_image() to convert and display images in RGB format compatible with Tkinter. The match_images() method manages keypoint detection, descriptor calculation using BRISK, descriptor matching with the Brute-Force Matcher, and visualization of matched keypoints with colored lines on canvas_frame. This comprehensive interface empowers users to explore and analyze image similarities based on distinct keypoints effectively.

The seventh project utilizes Tkinter to create a GUI application tailored for processing and analyzing video frames. It integrates various libraries such as Pillow, imageio, OpenCV, numpy, matplotlib, pywt, and os to support functionalities ranging from video handling to image processing and feature analysis. At its core is the Filter_CroppedFrame class, which manages the GUI layout and functionality. The application features control buttons for video playback, comboboxes for selecting zoom levels, filters, and matchers, and a canvas for displaying video frames with support for interactive navigation and frame processing. Event handlers facilitate tasks like video file loading, playback control, and frame navigation, while offering options for applying filters and feature matching algorithms to enhance video analysis capabilities.

CONTENT

SIFT IMAGE MATCHING	**1**
PURPOSE OF PROJECT	1
CLASS AND CONSTRUCTOR	3
LOADING AND DISPLAYING IMAGES	5
MATCHING IMAGES	7
ENTRY POINT	10
RUNNING PROGRAM	11
SOURCE CODE	13
ORB IMAGE MATCHING	**17**
PURPOSE OF PROJECT	17
CLASS AND CONSTRUCTOR	19
LOADING AND DISPLAYING IMAGES	22
MATCHING IMAGES	24
ENTRY POINT	28
RUNNING PROGRAM	28
SOURCE CODE	29
FAST IMAGE MATCHING	**33**
PURPOSE OF PROJECT	33
CLASS AND CONSTRUCTOR	35
LOADING AND DISPLAYING IMAGES	38
MATCHING IMAGES	40
ENTRY POINT	42
RUNNING PROGRAM	43
SOURCE CODE	44
AGAST IMAGE MATCHING	**47**

PURPOSE OF PROJECT	47
MATCHING IMAGES	49
RUNNING PROGRAM	50
SOURCE CODE	51
AKAZE IMAGE MATCHING	**55**
PURPOSE OF PROJECT	55
MATCHING IMAGES	56
RUNNING PROGRAM	58
SOURCE CODE	59
BRISK IMAGE MATCHING	**63**
PURPOSE OF PROJECT	63
MATCHING IMAGES	65
RUNNING PROGRAM	67
SOURCE CODE	68
MATCHING CROPPED OBJECT IN VIDEO	**71**
PURPOSE OF PROJECT	71
CLASS AND CONSTRUCTOR	73
CREATING WIDGETS	75
CONTROLLING VIDEO PLAYBACK	78
DISPLAYING AND UPDATING FRAME	80
NAVIGATING FRAMES	82
HANDLING MOUSE EVENTS	84
VISUALIZING HISTOGRAMS	87
UPDATING FILTER PARAMETERS	92
ACCESSING FILTERS PARAMETERS	98
DEFINING FILTERS	101
CHOOSING FILTER	106
GENERATING POPUP WINDOW	108
RUNNING DESCRIPTOR BASED IMAGES MATCHING	114
RUNNING PROGRAM	117
SOURCE CODE	124
BIBLIOGRAPHY	**146**

SIFT IMAGE MATCHING

PURPOSE OF PROJECT

The project is a sophisticated tool designed for comparing and matching visual features between two images using the Scale-Invariant Feature Transform (SIFT) algorithm. This project leverages advanced computer vision techniques to extract distinctive keypoints and descriptors from images, making it robust against variations in scale, rotation, and illumination. Its primary goal is to provide a user-friendly yet powerful interface for image matching tasks.

The project features a graphical user interface (GUI) built with Tkinter, which makes it accessible to users without extensive programming knowledge. The GUI includes buttons for loading images and controls for adjusting various parameters of the SIFT and BFMatcher algorithms. This design ensures that users can interact with the application intuitively, adjusting settings and viewing results directly, thereby enhancing usability.

Users can load two images into the application using the "Load Image 1" and "Load Image 2" buttons. The images are displayed side-by-side on a scrollable canvas, which allows users to easily view and compare them. This visual comparison is crucial for assessing differences and similarities between the images both before and after applying the SIFT matching process.

The application provides sliders and input fields for customizing the parameters of the SIFT algorithm, such as the number of features, octave layers, contrast threshold, edge threshold, and sigma. Users can also adjust BFMatcher settings, including the norm type and cross-check option. These customization options enable users to fine-tune the algorithm to achieve optimal matching results for different types of images.

The core functionality of the project involves detecting keypoints in the loaded images and computing their descriptors using the SIFT algorithm. Keypoints are distinctive points in the image that remain invariant to scale and rotation, making them suitable for reliable matching. Descriptors, on the other hand, are vectors that describe the local image patch around each keypoint, enabling detailed comparison of keypoints between images.

To find correspondences between the descriptors of the two images, the project employs the BFMatcher algorithm. BFMatcher (Brute Force Matcher) is a straightforward yet effective method for matching descriptors by comparing each descriptor in the first image with all descriptors in the second image. The application supports different norm types and the option for cross-checking matches, which enhances accuracy.

To further improve the reliability of the matches, the project implements a ratio test, a common technique in feature matching. This test filters out poor matches by ensuring that the distance of the best match is significantly smaller than that of the second-best match. This step helps in retaining only the most reliable correspondences between the images.

Once the matches are determined, the application draws lines between matching keypoints in the two images to visually represent the correspondences. The matched image is displayed on the same scrollable canvas, replacing the original images. This visual representation helps users easily understand and verify the matching results.

The project also allows users to adjust the thickness and color of the lines connecting matching keypoints, adding another layer of customization. This feature can be particularly useful for highlighting important matches or for better visual clarity in the final output.

Overall, SIFTMacher_NEW.py is a comprehensive tool designed to make the process of image matching accessible and efficient. By combining a user-friendly interface with powerful computer vision algorithms, it provides a versatile solution for tasks that require robust feature matching. Whether for academic research, industrial applications, or personal projects, this tool offers significant utility in the realm of image processing.

CLASS AND CONSTRUCTOR

The script is an application that uses the Scale-Invariant Feature Transform (SIFT) algorithm to compare and match features between two images. It utilizes the Tkinter library to create a graphical user interface (GUI) that allows users to load images, adjust SIFT parameters, and view the results of the image matching process. The application begins by importing necessary libraries including OpenCV for image processing, NumPy for numerical operations, Tkinter for the GUI, and PIL for image manipulation.

In the __init__() method of the SIFTMatcherApp class, the GUI is set up with various widgets. A control frame is created at the top of the window to hold buttons and other controls. Buttons are added to load two images and to match the images. Sliders and input fields are provided for adjusting SIFT parameters such as the number of features, octave layers, contrast threshold, edge threshold, and sigma. Similarly, parameters for the BFMatcher (Brute Force Matcher), such as norm type and cross-check option, can be adjusted using dropdown menus and entry fields.

The load_image1() and load_image2() methods allow users to select and load images from their file system. These images are then displayed on a canvas within the application. The canvas is scrollable, ensuring that users can view large images conveniently. When an image is loaded, it is converted to the appropriate color format using OpenCV and PIL, then displayed on the canvas with tags to differentiate between the two images.

The match_images() method is where the core functionality of the application lies. This method retrieves the user-specified SIFT parameters and initializes the SIFT detector. It then detects keypoints and computes descriptors for both images. Using the specified BFMatcher parameters, it matches the descriptors of the two images. A ratio test is applied to filter out poor matches, ensuring only the most reliable matches are retained. The method then draws lines between the matching keypoints on a combined image, visually representing the correspondences.

Finally, the matched image is displayed on the canvas, replacing the original images. This visual representation allows users to easily see and verify the matching results. Scrollbars are configured to ensure that the entire matched image can be viewed regardless of its size. Overall, the SIFTMacher_NEW.py script provides a comprehensive tool for feature matching in images, combining powerful computer vision techniques with an intuitive user interface.

```python
#SIFTMacher_NEW.py
import cv2
import numpy as np
from tkinter import Tk, Label, Button, filedialog, Canvas, Scale, Entry, StringVar, OptionMenu, HORIZONTAL, Scrollbar, RIGHT, BOTTOM, LEFT, Y, X
from PIL import Image, ImageTk

class SIFTMatcherApp:
    def __init__(self, root):
        self.root = root
        self.root.title("SIFT Image Matcher")

        # Frame for control widgets
        control_frame = Canvas(root)
        control_frame.pack(side="top", fill="x")

        self.load_button1 = Button(control_frame, text="Load Image 1", command=self.load_image1)
        self.load_button1.pack(side="left")

        self.load_button2 = Button(control_frame, text="Load Image 2", command=self.load_image2)
        self.load_button2.pack(side="left")

        self.match_button = Button(control_frame, text="Match Images", command=self.match_images)
        self.match_button.pack(side="left")

        # Parameters for SIFT
        Label(control_frame, text="nfeatures:").pack(side="left")
        self.nfeatures = Scale(control_frame, from_=0, to=10000, orient=HORIZONTAL)
        self.nfeatures.pack(side="left")

        Label(control_frame, text="nOctaveLayers:").pack(side="left")
        self.nOctaveLayers = Scale(control_frame, from_=1, to=10, orient=HORIZONTAL)
        self.nOctaveLayers.pack(side="left")

        Label(control_frame, text="contrastThreshold:").pack(side="left")
        self.contrastThreshold = Scale(control_frame, from_=0.01, to=0.1, resolution=0.01, orient=HORIZONTAL)
        self.contrastThreshold.pack(side="left")

        Label(control_frame, text="edgeThreshold:").pack(side="left")
        self.edgeThreshold = Scale(control_frame, from_=1, to=31, orient=HORIZONTAL)
        self.edgeThreshold.pack(side="left")

        Label(control_frame, text="sigma:").pack(side="left")
        self.sigma = Scale(control_frame, from_=0.8, to=2.0, resolution=0.1, orient=HORIZONTAL)
        self.sigma.pack(side="left")
```

```
    # Parameters for BFMatcher
    Label(control_frame, text="Norm Type:").pack(side="left")
    self.normType = StringVar(root)
    self.normType.set("NORM_L2")
    OptionMenu(control_frame, self.normType, "NORM_L1", "NORM_L2",
"NORM_HAMMING", "NORM_HAMMING2").pack(side="left")

    Label(control_frame, text="Cross Check:").pack(side="left")
    self.crossCheck = StringVar(root)
    self.crossCheck.set("False")
    OptionMenu(control_frame, self.crossCheck, "True", "False").pack(side="left")

    Label(control_frame, text="k:").pack(side="left")
    self.k = Entry(control_frame)
    self.k.insert(0, "2")
    self.k.pack(side="left")

    # Canvas with scrollbars
    self.canvas_frame = Canvas(root, width=1000, height=700)
    self.canvas_frame.pack(side="left", fill="both", expand=True)

    self.h_scrollbar = Scrollbar(root, orient="horizontal",
command=self.canvas_frame.xview)
    self.h_scrollbar.pack(side=BOTTOM, fill=X)

    self.v_scrollbar = Scrollbar(root, orient="vertical",
command=self.canvas_frame.yview)
    self.v_scrollbar.pack(side=RIGHT, fill=Y)

    self.canvas_frame.configure(xscrollcommand=self.h_scrollbar.set,
yscrollcommand=self.v_scrollbar.set)

    self.image1 = None
    self.image2 = None
    self.keypoints1 = None
    self.descriptors1 = None
    self.keypoints2 = None
    self.descriptors2 = None
```

LOADING AND DISPLAYING IMAGES

In the SIFTMacher_NEW.py script, the methods load_image1() and load_image2() handle the process of loading images into the application. These methods use the filedialog.askopenfilename() function from Tkinter to open a file dialog, allowing the user to select an image file from their computer. Once an image file is selected, it is read into the application using OpenCV's cv2.imread() function, which loads the image into a NumPy array.

The show_image() method is responsible for displaying the loaded image on the application's canvas. This method first checks if the image is grayscale (i.e., it has only two dimensions). If the image is grayscale, it converts the image to RGB format using cv2.cvtColor(image, cv2.COLOR_GRAY2RGB). If the image is already in RGB format, it converts it from BGR to RGB format (since OpenCV loads images in BGR format by default). The converted image is then transformed into a PIL image object using Image.fromarray(image_rgb) and subsequently converted into a format suitable for Tkinter display using ImageTk.PhotoImage(image_pil).

The show_image() method then displays the image on the canvas at the specified coordinates (x, y). The create_image() method of the canvas is used to place the image, and a tag (either 'image1' or 'image2') is assigned to it to differentiate between the two images. This tag is also used to dynamically create an attribute (e.g., image1_tk or image2_tk) using setattr, which helps in keeping a reference to the Tkinter image object to prevent it from being garbage collected.

Additionally, the show_image() method updates the scroll region of the canvas to ensure that the entire image can be viewed even if it is larger than the canvas dimensions. The config method of the canvas is called with the scrollregion parameter set to the bounding box of all elements on the canvas (self.canvas_frame.bbox("all")), enabling the scrollbars to adjust their range accordingly.

In summary, these methods work together to load images from the file system, convert them to the appropriate format for display, and render them on the application's canvas while ensuring the canvas is scrollable to accommodate large images. This functionality is crucial for allowing users to visually inspect and interact with the images before and after performing the SIFT matching process.

```python
def load_image1(self):
    file_path = filedialog.askopenfilename()
    if file_path:
        self.image1 = cv2.imread(file_path)
        self.show_image(self.image1, 0, 0, 'image1')

def load_image2(self):
    file_path = filedialog.askopenfilename()
    if file_path:
        self.image2 = cv2.imread(file_path)
        self.show_image(self.image2, 600, 0, 'image2')

def show_image(self, image, x, y, tag):
    if len(image.shape) == 2:
        # If the image is grayscale
        image_rgb = cv2.cvtColor(image, cv2.COLOR_GRAY2RGB)
    else:
```

```
        # If the image is already in RGB
        image_rgb = cv2.cvtColor(image, cv2.COLOR_BGR2RGB)
    image_pil = Image.fromarray(image_rgb)
    image_tk = ImageTk.PhotoImage(image_pil)
    self.canvas_frame.create_image(x, y, anchor="nw", image=image_tk, tags=tag)
    setattr(self, f"{tag}_tk", image_tk)

    # Update scroll region
    self.canvas_frame.config(scrollregion=self.canvas_frame.bbox("all"))
```

MATCHING IMAGES

The match_images() method in the SIFTMatcherApp class is designed to perform keypoint detection, descriptor extraction, and feature matching between two images loaded into the application. Initially, the method checks if both image1 and image2 are loaded. If either image is missing, it prints a message asking the user to load both images and exits. This check ensures that the subsequent operations have the necessary input images.

Next, the method retrieves user-defined parameters for the SIFT (Scale-Invariant Feature Transform) algorithm. These parameters include nfeatures, nOctaveLayers, contrastThreshold, edgeThreshold, and sigma. The parameters are obtained using the .get() method on various Tkinter widgets. These settings allow the user to customize the behavior of the SIFT algorithm to potentially enhance the accuracy and efficiency of keypoint detection and descriptor computation.

With the retrieved parameters, the method initializes the SIFT detector using cv2.SIFT_create(). This setup allows the SIFT detector to detect keypoints and compute descriptors for both images using the detectAndCompute() method. Keypoints are distinctive points in an image, and descriptors are vectors that describe the local image patches around these keypoints. The method then retrieves parameters for the BFMatcher (Brute-Force Matcher) from the user inputs, including normType, crossCheck, and k. The normType specifies the norm type for distance measurement, crossCheck indicates whether to perform cross-checking, and k specifies the number of nearest neighbors to find.

The BFMatcher is created with these parameters, and the knnMatch method is called to find the k nearest neighbors for each descriptor in image1 from the descriptors in image2. This method returns a list of matches for each descriptor, with each match being a list of k DMatch objects. Before proceeding with the matching, the method checks if the descriptors for both images are valid, ensuring they are not None and have the correct data type (np.float32). If the descriptors are invalid, it prints an error message and exits to prevent further issues.

To filter out good matches, the method applies a ratio test. It checks if the distance of the best match (m) is less than 75% of the distance of the second-best match (n). If this condition is met, the match is considered a good match and is added to the good_matches list. The method then uses cv2.drawMatches to draw the matches between the two images. The good_matches list is passed to this function along with the keypoints and images. The flags=cv2.DrawMatchesFlags_NOT_DRAW_SINGLE_POINTS flag ensures that only matches are drawn, not the keypoints without matches.

For better visibility, the method manually draws thicker lines between the matched keypoints. It iterates over the good_matches and retrieves the coordinates of the matched keypoints from both images. The coordinates from image2 are offset by the width of image1 to account for the combined image width. For each match, a random color is generated using np.random.randint, and cv2.line is used to draw lines between the matched keypoints on the matched_image with these random colors.

After drawing the matches, the matched_image is converted from BGR to RGB format using cv2.cvtColor, as OpenCV uses BGR by default, while PIL and Tkinter use RGB. The RGB image is then converted to a PIL image using Image.fromarray, making it compatible with Tkinter. This PIL image is further converted to a Tkinter-compatible image using ImageTk.PhotoImage.

Before displaying the new matched image, the method clears the canvas of any previously displayed images using delete("image1") and delete("image2"). This ensures the canvas is ready for the new image. The matched image is displayed on the canvas using create_image(), placing it at the top-left corner (0, 0) of the canvas with the tag "matched" for future reference. To prevent the Tkinter image from being garbage collected, it is stored as an attribute of the canvas (self.canvas_frame.image_matched). This step is necessary because Tkinter requires a reference to the image object to display it correctly. Finally, the method updates the scroll region of the canvas using config(scrollregion=self.canvas_frame.bbox("all")), ensuring that the scrollbars adjust to the size of the displayed image, allowing the user to scroll and view the entire matched image.

```python
    def match_images(self):
        if self.image1 is None or self.image2 is None:
            print("Please load both images first.")
            return

        # Get SIFT parameters from user inputs
        nfeatures = self.nfeatures.get()
        nOctaveLayers = self.nOctaveLayers.get()
        contrastThreshold = self.contrastThreshold.get()
        edgeThreshold = self.edgeThreshold.get()
        sigma = self.sigma.get()

        # Initialize the SIFT detector with user parameters
        sift = cv2.SIFT_create(
            nfeatures=nfeatures,
            nOctaveLayers=nOctaveLayers,
            contrastThreshold=contrastThreshold,
            edgeThreshold=edgeThreshold,
            sigma=sigma
        )

        # Detect keypoints and compute descriptors for both images
        self.keypoints1, self.descriptors1 = sift.detectAndCompute(self.image1, None)
        self.keypoints2, self.descriptors2 = sift.detectAndCompute(self.image2, None)

        # Get BFMatcher parameters from user inputs
        normType = getattr(cv2, self.normType.get())
        crossCheck = self.crossCheck.get() == "True"
        k = int(self.k.get())

        # Use BFMatcher to match descriptors with user parameters
        bf = cv2.BFMatcher(normType, crossCheck=crossCheck)
        # Check if descriptors are valid and have the correct type
        if self.descriptors1 is None or self.descriptors2 is None or self.descriptors1.dtype != np.float32 or self.descriptors2.dtype != np.float32:
            print("Error: Descriptors are not valid or not of type CV_32F.")
            return
        matches = bf.knnMatch(self.descriptors1, self.descriptors2, k=k)

        # Apply ratio test to filter good matches
        good_matches = []
        for match in matches:
            if len(match) == 2:
                m, n = match
                if m.distance < 0.75 * n.distance:
                    good_matches.append(m)

        # Draw top matches with thicker lines
        matched_image = cv2.drawMatches(self.image1, self.keypoints1, self.image2, self.keypoints2, good_matches, None, flags=cv2.DrawMatchesFlags_NOT_DRAW_SINGLE_POINTS)

        # Draw thicker lines manually
        for match in good_matches:
            img1_idx = match.queryIdx
            img2_idx = match.trainIdx
            (x1, y1) = self.keypoints1[img1_idx].pt
            (x2, y2) = self.keypoints2[img2_idx].pt
```

```
            x2 += self.image1.shape[1]  # Offset by width of image1 to account for
combined image width

            # Use random color for the lines (same as drawMatches)
            color = tuple(np.random.randint(0, 255, 3).tolist())
            cv2.line(matched_image, (int(x1), int(y1)), (int(x2), int(y2)), color, 2)

        # Convert matched_image to RGB
        matched_image_rgb = cv2.cvtColor(matched_image, cv2.COLOR_BGR2RGB)
        matched_image_pil = Image.fromarray(matched_image_rgb)
        matched_image_tk = ImageTk.PhotoImage(matched_image_pil)

        # Clear the canvas before displaying the matched image
        self.canvas_frame.delete("image1")
        self.canvas_frame.delete("image2")

        # Display matched image
        self.canvas_frame.create_image(0, 0, anchor="nw", image=matched_image_tk,
tags="matched")
        self.canvas_frame.image_matched = matched_image_tk

        # Update scroll region
        self.canvas_frame.config(scrollregion=self.canvas_frame.bbox("all"))
```

ENTRY POINT

The code within the if __name__ == "__main__": block serves as the entry point of the application. It initializes the Tkinter main window by creating an instance of Tk() and then creates an instance of the SIFTMatcherApp class, passing the main window (root) as an argument. Finally, it calls root.mainloop(), which starts the Tkinter event loop, keeping the application running and responsive to user inputs until the window is closed. This setup ensures that the GUI is correctly initialized and displayed to the user.

```
if __name__ == "__main__":
    root = Tk()
    app = SIFTMatcherApp(root)
    root.mainloop()
```

RUNNING PROGRAM

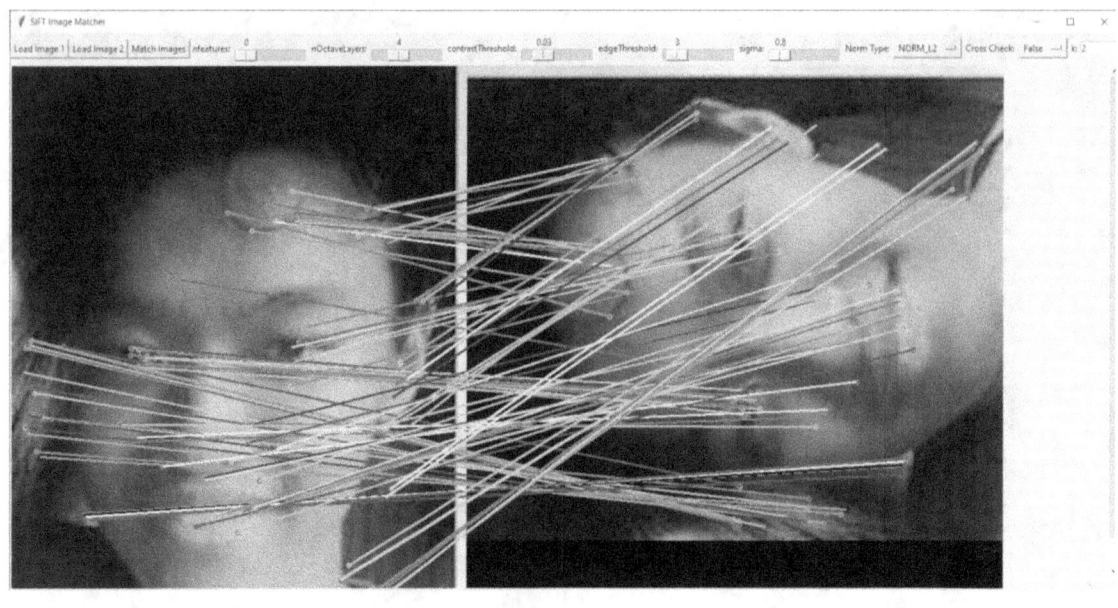

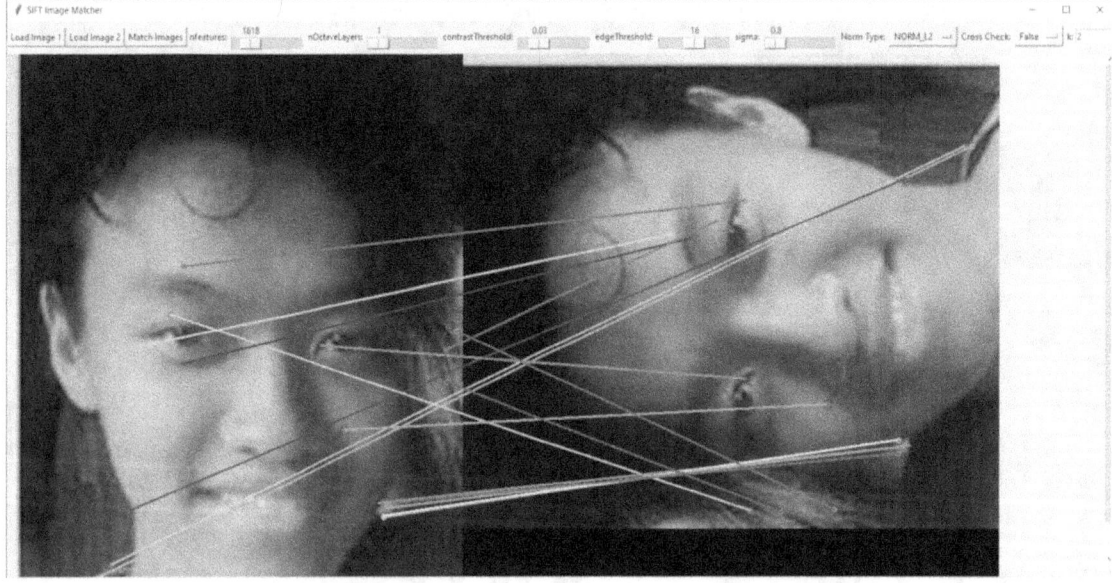

SOURCE CODE

```python
#SIFTMacher_NEW.py
import cv2
import numpy as np
from tkinter import Tk, Label, Button, filedialog, Canvas, Scale, Entry, StringVar, OptionMenu, HORIZONTAL, Scrollbar, RIGHT, BOTTOM, LEFT, Y, X
from PIL import Image, ImageTk

class SIFTMatcherApp:
    def __init__(self, root):
        self.root = root
        self.root.title("SIFT Image Matcher")

        # Frame for control widgets
        control_frame = Canvas(root)
        control_frame.pack(side="top", fill="x")

        self.load_button1 = Button(control_frame, text="Load Image 1", command=self.load_image1)
        self.load_button1.pack(side="left")

        self.load_button2 = Button(control_frame, text="Load Image 2", command=self.load_image2)
        self.load_button2.pack(side="left")

        self.match_button = Button(control_frame, text="Match Images", command=self.match_images)
        self.match_button.pack(side="left")

        # Parameters for SIFT
        Label(control_frame, text="nfeatures:").pack(side="left")
        self.nfeatures = Scale(control_frame, from_=0, to=10000, orient=HORIZONTAL)
        self.nfeatures.pack(side="left")

        Label(control_frame, text="nOctaveLayers:").pack(side="left")
        self.nOctaveLayers = Scale(control_frame, from_=1, to=10, orient=HORIZONTAL)
        self.nOctaveLayers.pack(side="left")

        Label(control_frame, text="contrastThreshold:").pack(side="left")
        self.contrastThreshold = Scale(control_frame, from_=0.01, to=0.1, resolution=0.01, orient=HORIZONTAL)
        self.contrastThreshold.pack(side="left")

        Label(control_frame, text="edgeThreshold:").pack(side="left")
        self.edgeThreshold = Scale(control_frame, from_=1, to=31, orient=HORIZONTAL)
        self.edgeThreshold.pack(side="left")

        Label(control_frame, text="sigma:").pack(side="left")
        self.sigma = Scale(control_frame, from_=0.8, to=2.0, resolution=0.1, orient=HORIZONTAL)
        self.sigma.pack(side="left")

        # Parameters for BFMatcher
        Label(control_frame, text="Norm Type:").pack(side="left")
        self.normType = StringVar(root)
```

```python
        self.normType.set("NORM_L2")
        OptionMenu(control_frame, self.normType, "NORM_L1", "NORM_L2",
"NORM_HAMMING", "NORM_HAMMING2").pack(side="left")

        Label(control_frame, text="Cross Check:").pack(side="left")
        self.crossCheck = StringVar(root)
        self.crossCheck.set("False")
        OptionMenu(control_frame, self.crossCheck, "True", "False").pack(side="left")

        Label(control_frame, text="k:").pack(side="left")
        self.k = Entry(control_frame)
        self.k.insert(0, "2")
        self.k.pack(side="left")

        # Canvas with scrollbars
        self.canvas_frame = Canvas(root, width=1000, height=700)
        self.canvas_frame.pack(side="left", fill="both", expand=True)

        self.h_scrollbar = Scrollbar(root, orient="horizontal",
command=self.canvas_frame.xview)
        self.h_scrollbar.pack(side=BOTTOM, fill=X)

        self.v_scrollbar = Scrollbar(root, orient="vertical",
command=self.canvas_frame.yview)
        self.v_scrollbar.pack(side=RIGHT, fill=Y)

        self.canvas_frame.configure(xscrollcommand=self.h_scrollbar.set,
yscrollcommand=self.v_scrollbar.set)

        self.image1 = None
        self.image2 = None
        self.keypoints1 = None
        self.descriptors1 = None
        self.keypoints2 = None
        self.descriptors2 = None

    def load_image1(self):
        file_path = filedialog.askopenfilename()
        if file_path:
            self.image1 = cv2.imread(file_path)
            self.show_image(self.image1, 0, 0, 'image1')

    def load_image2(self):
        file_path = filedialog.askopenfilename()
        if file_path:
            self.image2 = cv2.imread(file_path)
            self.show_image(self.image2, 600, 0, 'image2')

    def show_image(self, image, x, y, tag):
        if len(image.shape) == 2:
            # If the image is grayscale
            image_rgb = cv2.cvtColor(image, cv2.COLOR_GRAY2RGB)
        else:
            # If the image is already in RGB
            image_rgb = cv2.cvtColor(image, cv2.COLOR_BGR2RGB)
        image_pil = Image.fromarray(image_rgb)
        image_tk = ImageTk.PhotoImage(image_pil)
        self.canvas_frame.create_image(x, y, anchor="nw", image=image_tk, tags=tag)
```

```python
        setattr(self, f"{tag}_tk", image_tk)

    # Update scroll region
    self.canvas_frame.config(scrollregion=self.canvas_frame.bbox("all"))

def match_images(self):
    if self.image1 is None or self.image2 is None:
        print("Please load both images first.")
        return

    # Get SIFT parameters from user inputs
    nfeatures = self.nfeatures.get()
    nOctaveLayers = self.nOctaveLayers.get()
    contrastThreshold = self.contrastThreshold.get()
    edgeThreshold = self.edgeThreshold.get()
    sigma = self.sigma.get()

    # Initialize the SIFT detector with user parameters
    sift = cv2.SIFT_create(
        nfeatures=nfeatures,
        nOctaveLayers=nOctaveLayers,
        contrastThreshold=contrastThreshold,
        edgeThreshold=edgeThreshold,
        sigma=sigma
    )

    # Detect keypoints and compute descriptors for both images
    self.keypoints1, self.descriptors1 = sift.detectAndCompute(self.image1, None)
    self.keypoints2, self.descriptors2 = sift.detectAndCompute(self.image2, None)

    # Get BFMatcher parameters from user inputs
    normType = getattr(cv2, self.normType.get())
    crossCheck = self.crossCheck.get() == "True"
    k = int(self.k.get())

    # Use BFMatcher to match descriptors with user parameters
    bf = cv2.BFMatcher(normType, crossCheck=crossCheck)
    # Check if descriptors are valid and have the correct type
    if self.descriptors1 is None or self.descriptors2 is None or self.descriptors1.dtype != np.float32 or self.descriptors2.dtype != np.float32:
        print("Error: Descriptors are not valid or not of type CV_32F.")
        return
    matches = bf.knnMatch(self.descriptors1, self.descriptors2, k=k)

    # Apply ratio test to filter good matches
    good_matches = []
    for match in matches:
        if len(match) == 2:
            m, n = match
            if m.distance < 0.75 * n.distance:
                good_matches.append(m)

    # Draw top matches with thicker lines
    matched_image = cv2.drawMatches(self.image1, self.keypoints1, self.image2, self.keypoints2, good_matches, None, flags=cv2.DrawMatchesFlags_NOT_DRAW_SINGLE_POINTS)

    # Draw thicker lines manually
```

```python
        for match in good_matches:
            img1_idx = match.queryIdx
            img2_idx = match.trainIdx
            (x1, y1) = self.keypoints1[img1_idx].pt
            (x2, y2) = self.keypoints2[img2_idx].pt
            x2 += self.image1.shape[1]  # Offset by width of image1 to account for combined image width

            # Use random color for the lines (same as drawMatches)
            color = tuple(np.random.randint(0, 255, 3).tolist())
            cv2.line(matched_image, (int(x1), int(y1)), (int(x2), int(y2)), color, 2)

        # Convert matched_image to RGB
        matched_image_rgb = cv2.cvtColor(matched_image, cv2.COLOR_BGR2RGB)
        matched_image_pil = Image.fromarray(matched_image_rgb)
        matched_image_tk = ImageTk.PhotoImage(matched_image_pil)

        # Clear the canvas before displaying the matched image
        self.canvas_frame.delete("image1")
        self.canvas_frame.delete("image2")

        # Display matched image
        self.canvas_frame.create_image(0, 0, anchor="nw", image=matched_image_tk, tags="matched")
        self.canvas_frame.image_matched = matched_image_tk

        # Update scroll region
        self.canvas_frame.config(scrollregion=self.canvas_frame.bbox("all"))

if __name__ == "__main__":
    root = Tk()
    app = SIFTMatcherApp(root)
    root.mainloop()
```

ORB IMAGE MATCHING

PURPOSE OF PROJECT

The project ORBMacher.py is a graphical user interface (GUI) application designed for image matching using the ORB (Oriented FAST and Rotated BRIEF) algorithm. It is implemented using the Python programming language, utilizing libraries such as OpenCV for image processing, Tkinter for the GUI, and PIL for handling image formats. The application allows users to load two images, adjust ORB parameters, and match the images based on their keypoints and descriptors.

The class ORBMatcherApp is the main component of the application. When an instance of this class is created, it initializes the main window and sets up various control widgets. These widgets include buttons for loading images, a button for initiating the matching process, and various sliders and options for adjusting the parameters of the ORB algorithm. These parameters include the number of features, scale factor, number of levels, edge threshold, first level, WTA_K, score type, and patch size.

The load_image1 and load_image2 methods allow users to load the first and second images, respectively. These methods use a file dialog to select an image file and then read the image using OpenCV. The show_image method displays the loaded image on a canvas within the GUI. This method converts the image to RGB format if necessary and then uses PIL to create a format suitable for display in Tkinter.

The match_images method is the core functionality of the application. It begins by ensuring both images are loaded. It then retrieves the user-specified ORB parameters from the GUI and initializes an ORB detector with these parameters. The method proceeds to detect keypoints and compute descriptors for both images using the ORB detector.

Once the keypoints and descriptors are obtained, the method employs a BFMatcher (Brute Force Matcher) to match the descriptors of the two images. The BFMatcher uses the Hamming distance to find the best matches, and the matches are sorted by distance to identify the top matches. The top matches are then drawn on a combined image using OpenCV's drawMatches function.

The matched image is enhanced by manually drawing thicker lines between the corresponding keypoints of the two images. This involves iterating through the matches, retrieving the coordinates of the matched keypoints, and drawing lines between them using a random color for each match. The matched image is then converted to RGB format and displayed on the canvas within the GUI.

The application includes scrollbars to navigate the displayed images, making it user-friendly even when dealing with large images. The scrollbars are linked to the canvas to ensure smooth scrolling and proper alignment of the displayed content.

In the __main__ block, the application initializes the Tkinter main window, creates an instance of the ORBMatcherApp class, and starts the Tkinter event loop. This setup ensures that the GUI remains responsive and operational as users interact with it.

The application provides a robust tool for visualizing and understanding the performance of the ORB algorithm in matching keypoints between two images. Users can experiment with different parameter settings to observe how they affect the matching process, making it a valuable educational tool for those learning about feature detection and image matching.

Overall, ORBMacher.py is a well-structured application that combines the power of OpenCV for image processing with the flexibility of Tkinter for creating interactive GUIs. Its modular design, with separate methods for loading images, displaying images, and matching images, makes it easy to understand and extend. The inclusion of user-adjustable parameters allows for experimentation and fine-tuning, which is essential for tasks involving computer vision and image processing.

CLASS AND CONSTRUCTOR

The Python script ORBMacher.py creates a graphical user interface (GUI) application using Tkinter for image matching based on the ORB (Oriented FAST and Rotated BRIEF) algorithm, combined with image processing capabilities from OpenCV and PIL.

Firstly, it imports necessary libraries: cv2 for computer vision tasks, numpy for numerical operations, Tkinter for GUI components, and PIL for handling images.

The ORBMatcherApp class initializes the application within a Tkinter window (root). It sets the window title to "ORB Image Matcher" and constructs a canvas (control_frame) to hold various GUI widgets. These include buttons (load_button1, load_button2, match_button) for loading images and initiating image matching operations. Each button is associated with a command (load_image1(), load_image2(), match_images()) that handles user interactions.

Next, the GUI includes several scales (Scale widgets) and dropdown menus (OptionMenu) to adjust ORB algorithm parameters such as nfeatures, scaleFactor, nlevels, edgeThreshold, firstLevel, WTA_K, scoreType, and patchSize. These parameters influence the detection and matching of keypoints between images. Labels (Label widgets) are provided to describe each parameter, and they are arranged within the control_frame canvas for an organized layout.

The canvas_frame is a large canvas widget configured to display images and facilitate scrolling using horizontal and vertical scrollbars (h_scrollbar, v_scrollbar). This setup ensures that users can view and navigate through large images comfortably within the GUI.

The class initializes variables (image1, image2, keypoints1, descriptors1, keypoints2, descriptors2) to store image data and keypoints/descriptors computed during the matching process. These variables are initially set to None as placeholders.

The load_image1() and load_image2() methods utilize filedialog to prompt users to select images from their filesystem. Upon selection, the images are loaded using OpenCV's cv2.imread function, converted to a format compatible with Tkinter (ImageTk.PhotoImage), and displayed on the canvas_frame using the show_image method. This method ensures images are displayed correctly and updates the canvas's scroll region dynamically.

The match_images() method, triggered by the "Match Images" button, retrieves current parameter values from the GUI, initializes an ORB detector (orb), detects keypoints, computes descriptors using detectAndCompute from OpenCV, and matches keypoints using a Brute Force Matcher (bf). It sorts matches by distance, draws them on a combined image using cv2.drawMatches, and enhances visualization by manually drawing thicker lines between matched keypoints.

In the __main__ block, a Tk instance (root) is created to initialize the main window, and an instance of ORBMatcherApp is instantiated to launch the application. The mainloop() method of root ensures the GUI remains responsive, handling user interactions and events until the application window is closed.

Overall, ORBMacher.py combines an intuitive user interface with powerful image processing capabilities, enabling interactive exploration and visualization of image matching techniques based on the ORB algorithm. It serves as a practical tool for both learning and applying computer vision techniques in various image analysis tasks.

```
#ORBMacher.py
import cv2
import numpy as np
from tkinter import Tk, Label, Button, filedialog, Canvas, Scale, Entry, StringVar, OptionMenu, HORIZONTAL, Scrollbar, RIGHT, BOTTOM, LEFT, Y, X
from PIL import Image, ImageTk

class ORBMatcherApp:
    def __init__(self, root):
        self.root = root
        self.root.title("ORB Image Matcher")

        # Frame for control widgets
        control_frame = Canvas(root)
        control_frame.pack(side="top", fill="x")
```

```python
        self.load_button1 = Button(control_frame, text="Load Image 1", command=self.load_image1)
        self.load_button1.pack(side="left")

        self.load_button2 = Button(control_frame, text="Load Image 2", command=self.load_image2)
        self.load_button2.pack(side="left")

        self.match_button = Button(control_frame, text="Match Images", command=self.match_images)
        self.match_button.pack(side="left")

        # Parameters for ORB
        Label(control_frame, text="nfeatures:").pack(side="left")
        self.nfeatures = Scale(control_frame, from_=0, to=10000, orient=HORIZONTAL)
        self.nfeatures.pack(side="left")

        Label(control_frame, text="scaleFactor:").pack(side="left")
        self.scaleFactor = Scale(control_frame, from_=1.01, to=2.0, resolution=0.01, orient=HORIZONTAL)
        self.scaleFactor.pack(side="left")

        Label(control_frame, text="nlevels:").pack(side="left")
        self.nlevels = Scale(control_frame, from_=1, to=32, orient=HORIZONTAL)
        self.nlevels.pack(side="left")

        Label(control_frame, text="edgeThreshold:").pack(side="left")
        self.edgeThreshold = Scale(control_frame, from_=1, to=31, orient=HORIZONTAL)
        self.edgeThreshold.pack(side="left")

        Label(control_frame, text="firstLevel:").pack(side="left")
        self.firstLevel = Scale(control_frame, from_=0, to=255, orient=HORIZONTAL)
        self.firstLevel.pack(side="left")

        Label(control_frame, text="WTA_K:").pack(side="left")
        self.WTA_K = Scale(control_frame, from_=2, to=4, orient=HORIZONTAL)
        self.WTA_K.pack(side="left")

        Label(control_frame, text="scoreType:").pack(side="left")
        self.scoreType = StringVar(root)
        self.scoreType.set("HARRIS_SCORE")
        OptionMenu(control_frame, self.scoreType, "HARRIS_SCORE", "FAST_SCORE").pack(side="left")

        # Adjusted patchSize scale
        Label(control_frame, text="patchSize:").pack(side="left")
        self.patchSize = Scale(control_frame, from_=2, to=31, orient=HORIZONTAL)  # Adjusted minimum value
```

```
        self.patchSize.pack(side="left")
        
        # Canvas with scrollbars
        self.canvas_frame = Canvas(root, width=1000, height=700)
        self.canvas_frame.pack(side="left", fill="both", expand=True)
        
        self.h_scrollbar = Scrollbar(root, orient="horizontal", 
command=self.canvas_frame.xview)
        self.h_scrollbar.pack(side=BOTTOM, fill=X)
        
        self.v_scrollbar = Scrollbar(root, orient="vertical", 
command=self.canvas_frame.yview)
        self.v_scrollbar.pack(side=RIGHT, fill=Y)
        
        self.canvas_frame.configure(xscrollcommand=self.h_scrollbar.set, 
yscrollcommand=self.v_scrollbar.set)
        
        self.image1 = None
        self.image2 = None
        self.keypoints1 = None
        self.descriptors1 = None
        self.keypoints2 = None
        self.descriptors2 = None
```

LOADING AND DISPLAYING IMAGES

These methods in the ORBMatcherApp class facilitate the loading and display of images within a Tkinter-based graphical user interface (GUI). Here's a detailed explanation of each method:

load_image1(self)

This method is invoked when the user clicks the "Load Image 1" button. It opens a file dialog (filedialog.askopenfilename()) that allows the user to select an image file from their filesystem. If a file path (file_path) is returned (meaning the user selected a file), the method proceeds to load the image using OpenCV's cv2.imread(file_path). The loaded image is stored in self.image1. Subsequently, the show_image() method is called with self.image1, coordinates (0, 0), and the tag 'image1'. This method call displays image1 on the canvas (self.canvas_frame) at the top-left corner (0, 0).

load_image2(self)

Similar to load_image1(), this method handles the loading of the second image when the user clicks the "Load Image 2" button. It also opens a file dialog to select an image file

(file_path). If a valid file path is returned, the image is loaded using cv2.imread(file_path) and stored in self.image2. The show_image() method is then called with self.image2, coordinates (600, 0), and the tag 'image2'. This displays image2 on the canvas, starting at x-coordinate 600.

show_image(self, image, x, y, tag)

This utility method is responsible for displaying an image on the canvas (self.canvas_frame). It takes four parameters:
- image: The image to be displayed, which is expected to be a NumPy array representing the image data.
- x and y: The coordinates where the top-left corner of the image should be placed on the canvas.
- tag: A unique identifier for the image, used to manage and update the image later.

Inside show_image(), it first checks the shape of the image (image.shape). If the image is grayscale (i.e., it has only two dimensions), it converts it to RGB format using cv2.cvtColor(image, cv2.COLOR_GRAY2RGB). If the image is already in BGR (Blue-Green-Red) format (typically used by OpenCV for color images), it converts it to RGB using cv2.cvtColor(image, cv2.COLOR_BGR2RGB).

After converting the image to RGB, it creates a PIL Image object (Image.fromarray(image_rgb)) and then converts this PIL Image to a Tkinter-compatible format (ImageTk.PhotoImage(image_pil)). This Tkinter image object (image_tk) is then used to create an image on the canvas (self.canvas_frame.create_image(x, y, anchor="nw", image=image_tk, tags=tag)), positioned at coordinates (x, y) with the specified tag.

Furthermore, setattr(self, f"{tag}_tk", image_tk) dynamically assigns the Tkinter image object (image_tk) to an attribute of the instance (self.{tag}_tk). This allows easy access to the Tkinter image object associated with each image tag ('image1_tk' for image1 and 'image2_tk' for image2).

Lastly, self.canvas_frame.config(scrollregion=self.canvas_frame.bbox("all")) updates the scroll region of the canvas (self.canvas_frame) to encompass the bounding box (bbox) of all items on the canvas. This ensures that the canvas can be scrolled appropriately to view the entire image content if it exceeds the visible area.

Together, these methods provide a user-friendly interface to load, convert, and display images within a Tkinter application, making it easier to interactively work with image data and prepare for further processing or analysis.

```python
def load_image1(self):
    file_path = filedialog.askopenfilename()
    if file_path:
        self.image1 = cv2.imread(file_path)
        self.show_image(self.image1, 0, 0, 'image1')

def load_image2(self):
    file_path = filedialog.askopenfilename()
    if file_path:
        self.image2 = cv2.imread(file_path)
        self.show_image(self.image2, 600, 0, 'image2')

def show_image(self, image, x, y, tag):
    if len(image.shape) == 2:
        # If the image is grayscale
        image_rgb = cv2.cvtColor(image, cv2.COLOR_GRAY2RGB)
    else:
        # If the image is already in RGB
        image_rgb = cv2.cvtColor(image, cv2.COLOR_BGR2RGB)
    image_pil = Image.fromarray(image_rgb)
    image_tk = ImageTk.PhotoImage(image_pil)
    self.canvas_frame.create_image(x, y, anchor="nw", image=image_tk, tags=tag)
    setattr(self, f"{tag}_tk", image_tk)

    # Update scroll region
    self.canvas_frame.config(scrollregion=self.canvas_frame.bbox("all"))
```

MATCHING IMAGES

The match_images() method in the ORBMatcherApp class performs image matching using the ORB (Oriented FAST and Rotated BRIEF) feature detector and descriptor. Here's a detailed explanation of each part:

Method Overview

The match_images() method is called when the user clicks the "Match Images" button in the GUI. It starts by checking if both self.image1 and self.image2 are loaded (None). If either image is not loaded, it prints a message instructing the user to load both images and then returns, halting further execution.

ORB Parameter Initialization

Assuming both images are loaded, the method proceeds to retrieve various ORB algorithm parameters from the GUI widgets:

- nfeatures, scaleFactor, nlevels, edgeThreshold, firstLevel, WTA_K, and patchSize are obtained from respective Scale widgets. These parameters control aspects like the number of features to detect, image scale factor, number of pyramid levels, edge threshold, and more.
- scoreType determines the score calculation method used by ORB (cv2.ORB_HARRIS_SCORE or cv2.ORB_FAST_SCORE), based on the user's selection from an OptionMenu.

ORB Detector Initialization
Using the obtained parameters, an ORB detector (orb) is initialized via cv2.ORB_create(). This creates an ORB object configured with the user-defined parameters, which will be used to detect keypoints and compute descriptors for both images.

Keypoint Detection and Descriptor Computation
The ORB detector (orb) then processes self.image1 and self.image2:
- orb.detectAndCompute(self.image1, None) identifies keypoints (self.keypoints1) and computes descriptors (self.descriptors1) for image1.
- Similarly, it detects keypoints (self.keypoints2) and computes descriptors (self.descriptors2) for image2.

Descriptor Matching
To find correspondences between keypoints in the two images, a Brute Force Matcher (bf) is instantiated with cv2.BFMatcher(cv2.NORM_HAMMING, crossCheck=True). This matcher uses the Hamming distance metric to compare binary descriptors (self.descriptors1 and self.descriptors2). Setting crossCheck=True ensures that the match is symmetric (match from image1 to image2 should match back from image2 to image1).

Sorting Matches by Distance
The matches obtained from the matcher are sorted based on their distances (matches = sorted(matches, key=lambda x: x.distance)). Sorting helps to prioritize more accurate matches with smaller distances.

Drawing Matches
The top 10 matches (matches[:10]) are visualized using cv2.drawMatches(). This function draws lines between corresponding keypoints in image1 and image2, forming visual

connections. Before drawing, the method iterates over each match to retrieve the coordinates of matched keypoints and adjust the coordinates of keypoints in image2 to account for the width of image1.

Line Visualization
Each line connecting matched keypoints is drawn in a random color (color) using cv2.line(). This enhances the visibility of matched keypoints on the resultant image (matched_image), which initially combines image1 and image2 with drawn matches.

Image Conversion and Display
The matched_image() is converted from BGR to RGB format (cv2.cvtColor(matched_image, cv2.COLOR_BGR2RGB)) using OpenCV functions. This is followed by conversion to a PIL image (Image.fromarray(matched_image_rgb)) and then to a Tkinter-compatible format (ImageTk.PhotoImage(matched_image_pil)).

Updating Canvas Display
Before displaying the matched image on the GUI, the method clears any existing images tagged as 'image1' or 'image2' from self.canvas_frame using self.canvas_frame.delete("image1") and self.canvas_frame.delete("image2"). This ensures that only the matched image ("matched") is displayed.

Final Display and Scroll Region Update
The matched image (matched_image_tk) is then placed on self.canvas_frame at position (0, 0) with self.canvas_frame.create_image(0, 0, anchor="nw", image=matched_image_tk, tags="matched"). Finally, the scroll region of self.canvas_frame is updated to encompass the bounding box of all items on the canvas (self.canvas_frame.config(scrollregion=self.canvas_frame.bbox("all"))), enabling scrolling to view the entire matched image if it exceeds the visible area.

In summary, the match_images() method orchestrates the entire process of ORB feature detection, descriptor computation, matching, visualization, and GUI interaction, providing users with a visually enriched representation of matched keypoints between two loaded images.

```
def match_images(self):
    if self.image1 is None or self.image2 is None:
        print("Please load both images first.")
        return
```

```python
        # Get ORB parameters from user inputs
        nfeatures = self.nfeatures.get()
        scaleFactor = self.scaleFactor.get()
        nlevels = self.nlevels.get()
        edgeThreshold = self.edgeThreshold.get()
        firstLevel = self.firstLevel.get()
        WTA_K = self.WTA_K.get()
        scoreType = 0  # Default value

        if self.scoreType.get() == "HARRIS_SCORE":
            scoreType = cv2.ORB_HARRIS_SCORE
        elif self.scoreType.get() == "FAST_SCORE":
            scoreType = cv2.ORB_FAST_SCORE

        patchSize = self.patchSize.get()

        # Initialize the ORB detector with user parameters
        orb = cv2.ORB_create(
            nfeatures=nfeatures,
            scaleFactor=scaleFactor,
            nlevels=nlevels,
            edgeThreshold=edgeThreshold,
            firstLevel=firstLevel,
            WTA_K=WTA_K,
            scoreType=scoreType,
            patchSize=patchSize
        )

        # Detect keypoints and compute descriptors for both images
        self.keypoints1, self.descriptors1 = orb.detectAndCompute(self.image1, None)
        self.keypoints2, self.descriptors2 = orb.detectAndCompute(self.image2, None)

        # Use BFMatcher to match descriptors
        bf = cv2.BFMatcher(cv2.NORM_HAMMING, crossCheck=True)
        matches = bf.match(self.descriptors1, self.descriptors2)

        # Sort matches by distance
        matches = sorted(matches, key=lambda x: x.distance)

        # Draw top matches
        matched_image = cv2.drawMatches(self.image1, self.keypoints1, self.image2,
self.keypoints2, matches[:10], None,
flags=cv2.DrawMatchesFlags_NOT_DRAW_SINGLE_POINTS)

        # Draw thicker lines manually
        for match in matches:
            img1_idx = match.queryIdx
            img2_idx = match.trainIdx
            (x1, y1) = self.keypoints1[img1_idx].pt
            (x2, y2) = self.keypoints2[img2_idx].pt
            x2 += self.image1.shape[1]  # Offset by width of image1 to account for
combined image width

            # Use random color for the lines (same as drawMatches)
            color = tuple(np.random.randint(0, 255, 3).tolist())
            cv2.line(matched_image, (int(x1), int(y1)), (int(x2), int(y2)), color, 2)
```

```
        # Convert matched_image to RGB
        matched_image_rgb = cv2.cvtColor(matched_image, cv2.COLOR_BGR2RGB)
        matched_image_pil = Image.fromarray(matched_image_rgb)
        matched_image_tk = ImageTk.PhotoImage(matched_image_pil)

        # Clear the canvas before displaying the matched image
        self.canvas_frame.delete("image1")
        self.canvas_frame.delete("image2")

        # Display matched image
        self.canvas_frame.create_image(0, 0, anchor="nw", image=matched_image_tk, 
tags="matched")
        self.canvas_frame.image_matched = matched_image_tk

        # Update scroll region
        self.canvas_frame.config(scrollregion=self.canvas_frame.bbox("all"))
```

ENTRY POINT

```
if __name__ == "__main__":
    root = Tk()
    app = ORBMatcherApp(root)
    root.mainloop()
```

RUNNING PROGRAM

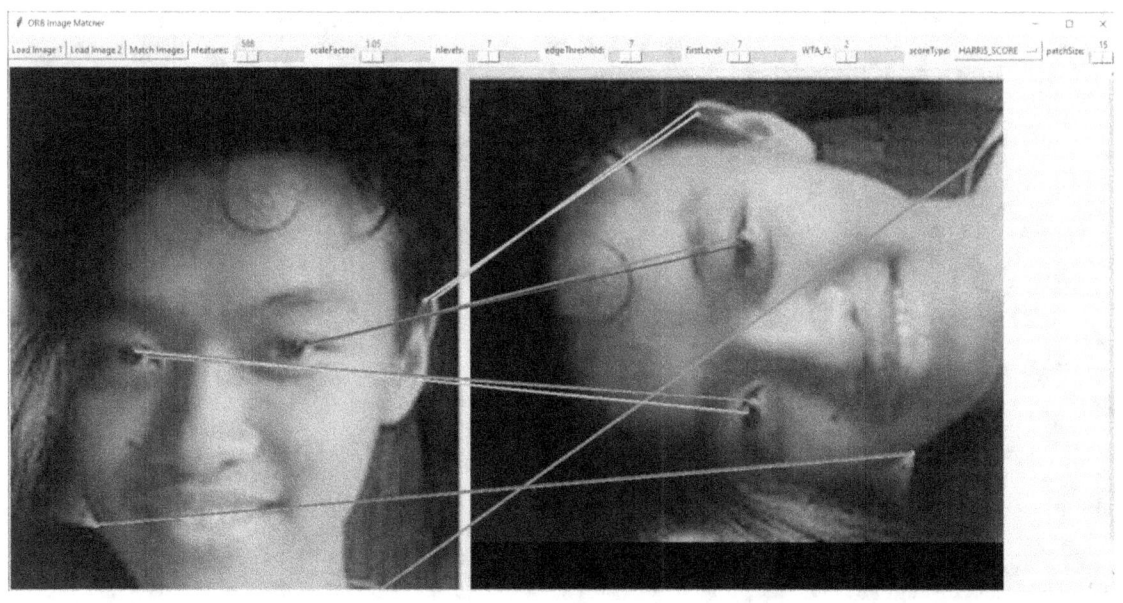

SOURCE CODE

```
#ORBMacher.py
import cv2
import numpy as np
from tkinter import Tk, Label, Button, filedialog, Canvas, Scale, Entry, StringVar, 
OptionMenu, HORIZONTAL, Scrollbar, RIGHT, BOTTOM, LEFT, Y, X
from PIL import Image, ImageTk

class ORBMatcherApp:
    def __init__(self, root):
        self.root = root
        self.root.title("ORB Image Matcher")

        # Frame for control widgets
        control_frame = Canvas(root)
        control_frame.pack(side="top", fill="x")

        self.load_button1 = Button(control_frame, text="Load Image 1", 
command=self.load_image1)
        self.load_button1.pack(side="left")

        self.load_button2 = Button(control_frame, text="Load Image 2", 
command=self.load_image2)
        self.load_button2.pack(side="left")

        self.match_button = Button(control_frame, text="Match Images", 
command=self.match_images)
        self.match_button.pack(side="left")

        # Parameters for ORB
```

```python
        Label(control_frame, text="nfeatures:").pack(side="left")
        self.nfeatures = Scale(control_frame, from_=0, to=10000, orient=HORIZONTAL)
        self.nfeatures.pack(side="left")

        Label(control_frame, text="scaleFactor:").pack(side="left")
        self.scaleFactor = Scale(control_frame, from_=1.01, to=2.0, resolution=0.01, orient=HORIZONTAL)
        self.scaleFactor.pack(side="left")

        Label(control_frame, text="nlevels:").pack(side="left")
        self.nlevels = Scale(control_frame, from_=1, to=32, orient=HORIZONTAL)
        self.nlevels.pack(side="left")

        Label(control_frame, text="edgeThreshold:").pack(side="left")
        self.edgeThreshold = Scale(control_frame, from_=1, to=31, orient=HORIZONTAL)
        self.edgeThreshold.pack(side="left")

        Label(control_frame, text="firstLevel:").pack(side="left")
        self.firstLevel = Scale(control_frame, from_=0, to=255, orient=HORIZONTAL)
        self.firstLevel.pack(side="left")

        Label(control_frame, text="WTA_K:").pack(side="left")
        self.WTA_K = Scale(control_frame, from_=2, to=4, orient=HORIZONTAL)
        self.WTA_K.pack(side="left")

        Label(control_frame, text="scoreType:").pack(side="left")
        self.scoreType = StringVar(root)
        self.scoreType.set("HARRIS_SCORE")
        OptionMenu(control_frame, self.scoreType, "HARRIS_SCORE", "FAST_SCORE").pack(side="left")

        # Adjusted patchSize scale
        Label(control_frame, text="patchSize:").pack(side="left")
        self.patchSize = Scale(control_frame, from_=2, to=31, orient=HORIZONTAL)  # Adjusted minimum value
        self.patchSize.pack(side="left")

        # Canvas with scrollbars
        self.canvas_frame = Canvas(root, width=1000, height=700)
        self.canvas_frame.pack(side="left", fill="both", expand=True)

        self.h_scrollbar = Scrollbar(root, orient="horizontal", command=self.canvas_frame.xview)
        self.h_scrollbar.pack(side=BOTTOM, fill=X)

        self.v_scrollbar = Scrollbar(root, orient="vertical", command=self.canvas_frame.yview)
        self.v_scrollbar.pack(side=RIGHT, fill=Y)

        self.canvas_frame.configure(xscrollcommand=self.h_scrollbar.set, yscrollcommand=self.v_scrollbar.set)

        self.image1 = None
        self.image2 = None
        self.keypoints1 = None
        self.descriptors1 = None
        self.keypoints2 = None
        self.descriptors2 = None
```

```python
def load_image1(self):
    file_path = filedialog.askopenfilename()
    if file_path:
        self.image1 = cv2.imread(file_path)
        self.show_image(self.image1, 0, 0, 'image1')

def load_image2(self):
    file_path = filedialog.askopenfilename()
    if file_path:
        self.image2 = cv2.imread(file_path)
        self.show_image(self.image2, 600, 0, 'image2')

def show_image(self, image, x, y, tag):
    if len(image.shape) == 2:
        # If the image is grayscale
        image_rgb = cv2.cvtColor(image, cv2.COLOR_GRAY2RGB)
    else:
        # If the image is already in RGB
        image_rgb = cv2.cvtColor(image, cv2.COLOR_BGR2RGB)
    image_pil = Image.fromarray(image_rgb)
    image_tk = ImageTk.PhotoImage(image_pil)
    self.canvas_frame.create_image(x, y, anchor="nw", image=image_tk, tags=tag)
    setattr(self, f"{tag}_tk", image_tk)

    # Update scroll region
    self.canvas_frame.config(scrollregion=self.canvas_frame.bbox("all"))

def match_images(self):
    if self.image1 is None or self.image2 is None:
        print("Please load both images first.")
        return

    # Get ORB parameters from user inputs
    nfeatures = self.nfeatures.get()
    scaleFactor = self.scaleFactor.get()
    nlevels = self.nlevels.get()
    edgeThreshold = self.edgeThreshold.get()
    firstLevel = self.firstLevel.get()
    WTA_K = self.WTA_K.get()
    scoreType = 0  # Default value

    if self.scoreType.get() == "HARRIS_SCORE":
        scoreType = cv2.ORB_HARRIS_SCORE
    elif self.scoreType.get() == "FAST_SCORE":
        scoreType = cv2.ORB_FAST_SCORE

    patchSize = self.patchSize.get()

    # Initialize the ORB detector with user parameters
    orb = cv2.ORB_create(
        nfeatures=nfeatures,
        scaleFactor=scaleFactor,
        nlevels=nlevels,
        edgeThreshold=edgeThreshold,
        firstLevel=firstLevel,
        WTA_K=WTA_K,
        scoreType=scoreType,
```

```python
            patchSize=patchSize
        )

        # Detect keypoints and compute descriptors for both images
        self.keypoints1, self.descriptors1 = orb.detectAndCompute(self.image1, None)
        self.keypoints2, self.descriptors2 = orb.detectAndCompute(self.image2, None)

        # Use BFMatcher to match descriptors
        bf = cv2.BFMatcher(cv2.NORM_HAMMING, crossCheck=True)
        matches = bf.match(self.descriptors1, self.descriptors2)

        # Sort matches by distance
        matches = sorted(matches, key=lambda x: x.distance)

        # Draw top matches
        matched_image = cv2.drawMatches(self.image1, self.keypoints1, self.image2, self.keypoints2, matches[:10], None, flags=cv2.DrawMatchesFlags_NOT_DRAW_SINGLE_POINTS)

        # Draw thicker lines manually
        for match in matches:
            img1_idx = match.queryIdx
            img2_idx = match.trainIdx
            (x1, y1) = self.keypoints1[img1_idx].pt
            (x2, y2) = self.keypoints2[img2_idx].pt
            x2 += self.image1.shape[1]  # Offset by width of image1 to account for combined image width

            # Use random color for the lines (same as drawMatches)
            color = tuple(np.random.randint(0, 255, 3).tolist())
            cv2.line(matched_image, (int(x1), int(y1)), (int(x2), int(y2)), color, 2)

        # Convert matched_image to RGB
        matched_image_rgb = cv2.cvtColor(matched_image, cv2.COLOR_BGR2RGB)
        matched_image_pil = Image.fromarray(matched_image_rgb)
        matched_image_tk = ImageTk.PhotoImage(matched_image_pil)

        # Clear the canvas before displaying the matched image
        self.canvas_frame.delete("image1")
        self.canvas_frame.delete("image2")

        # Display matched image
        self.canvas_frame.create_image(0, 0, anchor="nw", image=matched_image_tk, tags="matched")
        self.canvas_frame.image_matched = matched_image_tk

        # Update scroll region
        self.canvas_frame.config(scrollregion=self.canvas_frame.bbox("all"))

if __name__ == "__main__":
    root = Tk()
    app = ORBMatcherApp(root)
    root.mainloop()
```

FAST IMAGE MATCHING

PURPOSE OF PROJECT

The FASTMatcher.py script is a Python application built for comparing and visualizing keypoint matches between two images using computer vision techniques. It utilizes the FAST (Features from Accelerated Segment Test) feature detector along with the SIFT (Scale-Invariant Feature Transform) descriptor to achieve this functionality. The script is structured around a graphical user interface (GUI) created using the Tkinter library, designed to facilitate user interaction and display results in real-time.

Upon execution, the script initializes a Tkinter window titled "FAST Image Matcher". This window contains a control frame (control_frame) positioned at the top, which houses several interactive components. These include buttons for loading two images and a button to initiate the matching process between these images.

The "Load Image 1" and "Load Image 2" buttons trigger file dialogs when clicked, allowing users to select image files from their local system. Once an image file is selected, it is loaded using OpenCV (cv2.imread()) and displayed within the main canvas (canvas_frame) using the show_image() method. This method ensures that images are properly converted to RGB format if necessary before display.

The control frame also features parameter controls that affect the FAST detector:

- The threshold scale enables users to adjust the threshold value used in the FAST feature detection algorithm, influencing the sensitivity of keypoint detection.
- An option menu (nonmaxSuppression) provides a choice between enabling or disabling non-maximum suppression during keypoint detection, which affects how keypoints are selected and filtered.

The main canvas (canvas_frame) is a central component of the GUI, sized to accommodate images and matches with horizontal and vertical scrollbars (h_scrollbar and v_scrollbar) for navigation. This setup ensures that users can interactively explore images and their associated keypoints and matches, even if they extend beyond the initial viewable area.

The core functionality of the application resides in the match_images() method, which is invoked when the "Match Images" button is clicked. This method performs several essential tasks:
- It checks whether both self.image1 and self.image2 have been loaded. If not, it prompts the user to load both images before proceeding further.
- Key parameters for the FAST detector (threshold and nonmaxSuppression) are retrieved from the GUI controls to configure the detector accordingly.
- Using these parameters, the FAST detector (cv2.FastFeatureDetector_create()) identifies keypoints (keypoints1 and keypoints2) in both loaded images.
- The SIFT descriptor (cv2.SIFT_create()) is then employed to compute descriptors (descriptors1 and descriptors2) for the detected keypoints in each image.
- To establish matches between the descriptors, a Brute Force Matcher (cv2.BFMatcher) with the L2 norm distance metric is utilized (crossCheck=True). This step determines which keypoints in one image correspond to keypoints in the other image.
- Matches are sorted based on their distance to visualize the most relevant matches first. These matches are then drawn onto a new image (matched_image) using cv2.drawMatches(), which visually connects corresponding keypoints between the two images with colored lines.

Furthermore, to enhance the visibility of these matches, thicker lines are manually drawn between keypoints in the matched_image. Each line is assigned a random color to differentiate between different matches visually.

Once the matches are visualized, the matched_image is converted from BGR to RGB format using OpenCV (cv2.cvtColor()) and PIL (Image.fromarray()), ensuring compatibility with Tkinter for display. The resulting image (matched_image_tk) is then displayed on the canvas_frame using create_image(), replacing any previously displayed images ("image1" and "image2") to focus solely on the matched results.

Finally, the scroll region of canvas_frame is updated (self.canvas_frame.config(scrollregion=self.canvas_frame.bbox("all"))) to accommodate the new content dimensions, allowing users to scroll and view the entire matched image.

In summary, FASTMatcher.py provides a user-friendly interface for exploring and analyzing keypoint matches between two images using the FAST feature detector and SIFT descriptor. It combines interactive image loading, parameter adjustment, real-time matching visualization, and scrollable canvas functionality to facilitate comprehensive image analysis tasks in computer vision applications.

CLASS AND CONSTRUCTOR

The FASTMatcher.py script is a graphical application designed to help users load two images, detect keypoints in these images using the FAST (Features from Accelerated Segment Test) algorithm, match these keypoints, and visualize the matches. The code begins by importing essential libraries. OpenCV (cv2) is used for image processing and keypoint detection, NumPy (np) is used for numerical operations, Tkinter is used for creating the graphical user interface (GUI), and the PIL library (Image and ImageTk) is used for handling and displaying images within Tkinter.

The main class, FASTMatcherApp, is defined to encapsulate the application's functionality. The __init__() method initializes the class with a root window, sets the window title to "FAST Image Matcher," and creates a control frame at the top of the window to hold various control widgets. These widgets include buttons for loading images and matching keypoints, as well as sliders and option menus for adjusting FAST parameters.

The load_button1 and load_button2 buttons allow users to load two images. When clicked, these buttons trigger the load_image1() and load_image2() methods, respectively. These methods open a file dialog to let users select an image file, read the image using OpenCV, and display the image on a canvas.

The control frame also includes a slider for adjusting the FAST threshold parameter, which determines the sensitivity of the keypoint detection, and an option menu for enabling or disabling non-maximal suppression, which helps in refining the detected keypoints.

A canvas with horizontal and vertical scrollbars is created to display the images and their matches. This canvas is configured to update its scroll region based on the images displayed, ensuring users can navigate larger images if necessary.

The match_images() method is the core of the application's functionality. It first checks if both images have been loaded. If not, it prompts the user to load both images. It then retrieves the FAST parameters set by the user, initializes the FAST detector with these parameters, and detects keypoints in both images.

After detecting keypoints, the method uses the SIFT (Scale-Invariant Feature Transform) algorithm to compute descriptors for these keypoints. The descriptors are then matched using the BFMatcher (Brute-Force Matcher) with L2 norm, which is suitable for SIFT descriptors.

The matches are sorted based on distance to prioritize the best matches, and the top matches are visualized by drawing lines between corresponding keypoints in the two images. The cv2.drawMatches function is used to create an image showing the matches, and thicker lines are manually drawn for better visibility.

The matched image is converted from BGR to RGB format (as required by PIL) and displayed on the canvas. The original images are cleared from the canvas to make room for the matched image.

Finally, the script includes a main block that initializes the Tkinter root window, creates an instance of FASTMatcherApp, and starts the Tkinter main loop to run the application. This allows users to interact with the application, load images, adjust parameters, and visualize keypoint matches seamlessly.

```
#FASTMatcher.py
import cv2
import numpy as np
from tkinter import Tk, Label, Button, filedialog, Canvas, Scale, Entry, StringVar, 
OptionMenu, HORIZONTAL, Scrollbar, RIGHT, BOTTOM, LEFT, Y, X
from PIL import Image, ImageTk
```

```python
class FASTMatcherApp:
    def __init__(self, root):
        self.root = root
        self.root.title("FAST Image Matcher")

        # Frame for control widgets
        control_frame = Canvas(root)
        control_frame.pack(side="top", fill="x")

        self.load_button1 = Button(control_frame, text="Load Image 1", command=self.load_image1)
        self.load_button1.pack(side="left")

        self.load_button2 = Button(control_frame, text="Load Image 2", command=self.load_image2)
        self.load_button2.pack(side="left")

        self.match_button = Button(control_frame, text="Match Images", command=self.match_images)
        self.match_button.pack(side="left")

        # Parameters for FAST
        Label(control_frame, text="Threshold:").pack(side="left")
        self.threshold = Scale(control_frame, from_=0, to=255, orient=HORIZONTAL)
        self.threshold.pack(side="left")

        Label(control_frame, text="Nonmax Suppression:").pack(side="left")
        self.nonmaxSuppression = StringVar(root)
        self.nonmaxSuppression.set("True")
        OptionMenu(control_frame, self.nonmaxSuppression, "True", "False").pack(side="left")

        # Canvas with scrollbars
        self.canvas_frame = Canvas(root, width=1400, height=700)
        self.canvas_frame.pack(side="left", fill="both", expand=True)

        self.h_scrollbar = Scrollbar(root, orient="horizontal", command=self.canvas_frame.xview)
        self.h_scrollbar.pack(side=BOTTOM, fill=X)

        self.v_scrollbar = Scrollbar(root, orient="vertical", command=self.canvas_frame.yview)
        self.v_scrollbar.pack(side=RIGHT, fill=Y)

        self.canvas_frame.configure(xscrollcommand=self.h_scrollbar.set, yscrollcommand=self.v_scrollbar.set)

        self.image1 = None
        self.image2 = None
        self.keypoints1 = None
        self.descriptors1 = None
        self.keypoints2 = None
        self.descriptors2 = None
```

LOADING AND DISPLAYING IMAGES

Let's break down each function and its purpose in the context of this GUI application:

load_image1() Method

The load_image1() method is responsible for loading the first image.
- File Dialog: The method uses filedialog.askopenfilename() to open a file dialog where the user can select an image file from their file system.
- Read Image: If a file is selected (if file_path:), it reads the image using OpenCV's cv2.imread() function and assigns it to self.image1.
- Display Image: The method then calls self.show_image with the loaded image, specifying the coordinates (0, 0) and a tag 'image1' to display the image on the canvas.

load_image2() Method

The load_image2() method functions similarly to load_image1, but it is responsible for loading the second image.
- File Dialog: It opens a file dialog for the user to select an image file.
- Read Image: If a file is selected, it reads the image and assigns it to self.image2.
- Display Image: The method then calls self.show_image with the loaded image, specifying the coordinates (600, 0) and a tag 'image2' to display the image on the canvas.

show_image() Method

The show_image() method is responsible for displaying an image on the canvas at specified coordinates.
- Check Image Format: It first checks the format of the image. If the image is grayscale (i.e., has only 2 dimensions), it converts it to RGB format using cv2.cvtColor(image, cv2.COLOR_GRAY2RGB). If the image is already in RGB format, it converts it from BGR to RGB using cv2.cvtColor(image, cv2.COLOR_BGR2RGB).
- Convert to PIL Image: The method then converts the OpenCV image (in NumPy array format) to a PIL image using Image.fromarray(image_rgb).
- Convert to Tkinter Image: It then converts the PIL image to a format that Tkinter can display using ImageTk.PhotoImage(image_pil).

- Display on Canvas: The method uses the self.canvas_frame.create_image method to display the image on the canvas at the specified (x, y) coordinates, with the specified tag. The anchor="nw" parameter ensures the image is anchored at the top-left corner.
- Keep Reference: The setattr(self, f"{tag}_tk", image_tk) line ensures the Tkinter image object is stored as an attribute of the class. This is necessary to keep a reference to the image object to prevent it from being garbage collected.
- Update Scroll Region: Finally, the method updates the scroll region of the canvas to ensure the entire image is within the scrollable area using self.canvas_frame.config(scrollregion=self.canvas_frame.bbox("all")).

Summary

In summary, the load_image1() and load_image2() methods are used to load two different images into the application. The show_image() method handles the display of these images on the canvas, converting them from OpenCV's format to a format suitable for Tkinter. This setup allows the user to load and view two images side-by-side on a scrollable canvas.

```python
def load_image1(self):
    file_path = filedialog.askopenfilename()
    if file_path:
        self.image1 = cv2.imread(file_path)
        self.show_image(self.image1, 0, 0, 'image1')

def load_image2(self):
    file_path = filedialog.askopenfilename()
    if file_path:
        self.image2 = cv2.imread(file_path)
        self.show_image(self.image2, 600, 0, 'image2')

def show_image(self, image, x, y, tag):
    if len(image.shape) == 2:
        # If the image is grayscale
        image_rgb = cv2.cvtColor(image, cv2.COLOR_GRAY2RGB)
    else:
        # If the image is already in RGB
        image_rgb = cv2.cvtColor(image, cv2.COLOR_BGR2RGB)
    image_pil = Image.fromarray(image_rgb)
    image_tk = ImageTk.PhotoImage(image_pil)
    self.canvas_frame.create_image(x, y, anchor="nw", image=image_tk, tags=tag)
    setattr(self, f"{tag}_tk", image_tk)

    # Update scroll region
    self.canvas_frame.config(scrollregion=self.canvas_frame.bbox("all"))
```

MATCHING IMAGES

The match_images() method is a crucial part of the FASTMatcherApp class, responsible for detecting and matching keypoints between two loaded images. Here's an explanation of what each part of the code does:

1. Check Images Loaded: The method starts by checking if both images have been loaded. If either self.image1 or self.image2 is None, it prints a message and returns early, ensuring that subsequent operations are only performed when both images are available.
2. Get User Parameters: It retrieves user-specified parameters for the FAST keypoint detector. The threshold is obtained from a scale widget, and nonmaxSuppression is determined based on a boolean selection from an option menu.
3. Initialize FAST Detector: The method initializes a FAST (Features from Accelerated Segment Test) detector using OpenCV's cv2.FastFeatureDetector_create(), passing in the threshold and nonmaxSuppression parameters.
4. Detect Keypoints: Using the FAST detector, it detects keypoints in both images (self.image1 and self.image2) and stores the resulting keypoints in keypoints1 and keypoints2.
5. Compute Descriptors: To compute descriptors for the detected keypoints, the method initializes a SIFT (Scale-Invariant Feature Transform) detector. It then uses SIFT's compute() function to compute descriptors for the keypoints in both images, storing them in descriptors1 and descriptors2.
6. Match Descriptors: The method initializes a brute-force matcher (cv2.BFMatcher) with cv2.NORM_L2 norm type and cross-check enabled. It uses this matcher to find matches between the descriptors of the two images, storing the matches in a list.
7. Sort Matches: The matches are sorted by distance, which helps in identifying the best matches first. The sorted() function with a lambda function sorts the matches based on their distance attribute.
8. Draw Matches: Using cv2.drawMatches(), the method draws the top 10 matches between the keypoints of the two images on a single image (matched_image). This function visualizes the matching keypoints by drawing lines between them.
9. Draw Thicker Lines: For further emphasis, the method manually draws thicker lines between the matched keypoints. It iterates over the top 10 matches, extracts the coordinates of the matching keypoints, and uses cv2.line() to draw lines between them in random colors.

10. Display Matched Image: Finally, the method prepares the matched image for display. It converts the OpenCV image (in BGR format) to an RGB image, then to a PIL image, and then to a Tkinter-compatible image format. It clears the previous images from the canvas and displays the matched image. The scroll region of the canvas is updated to ensure the entire image is within the scrollable area.

This method effectively integrates the key aspects of image processing and graphical interface management, allowing users to visually compare and analyze keypoints between two images within the GUI.

```
def match_images(self):
    if self.image1 is None or self.image2 is None:
        print("Please load both images first.")
        return

    # Get FAST parameters from user inputs
    threshold = self.threshold.get()
    nonmaxSuppression = True if self.nonmaxSuppression.get() == "True" else False

    # Initialize the FAST detector with user parameters
    fast            =            cv2.FastFeatureDetector_create(threshold=threshold, nonmaxSuppression=nonmaxSuppression)

    # Detect keypoints for both images
    keypoints1 = fast.detect(self.image1, None)
    keypoints2 = fast.detect(self.image2, None)

    # Compute descriptors for keypoints
    sift = cv2.SIFT_create()
    keypoints1, descriptors1 = sift.compute(self.image1, keypoints1)
    keypoints2, descriptors2 = sift.compute(self.image2, keypoints2)

    # Use BFMatcher to match descriptors
    bf = cv2.BFMatcher(cv2.NORM_L2, crossCheck=True)
    matches = bf.match(descriptors1, descriptors2)

    # Sort matches by distance
    matches = sorted(matches, key=lambda x: x.distance)

    # Draw lines between matched keypoints
    matched_image    =    cv2.drawMatches(self.image1,    keypoints1,    self.image2, keypoints2, matches[:10], None, flags=cv2.DrawMatchesFlags_NOT_DRAW_SINGLE_POINTS)

    # Draw thicker lines manually
    for match in matches[:10]:
        img1_idx = match.queryIdx
        img2_idx = match.trainIdx
        (x1, y1) = keypoints1[img1_idx].pt
        (x2, y2) = keypoints2[img2_idx].pt
        x2 += self.image1.shape[1]  # Offset by width of image1 to account for combined image width
```

```python
            # Use random color for the lines (same as drawMatches)
            color = tuple(np.random.randint(0, 255, 3).tolist())
            cv2.line(matched_image, (int(x1), int(y1)), (int(x2), int(y2)), color, 2)

        # Convert matched_image to RGB
        matched_image_rgb = cv2.cvtColor(matched_image, cv2.COLOR_BGR2RGB)
        matched_image_pil = Image.fromarray(matched_image_rgb)
        matched_image_tk = ImageTk.PhotoImage(matched_image_pil)

        # Clear the canvas before displaying the matched image
        self.canvas_frame.delete("image1")
        self.canvas_frame.delete("image2")

        # Display matched image
        self.canvas_frame.create_image(0, 0, anchor="nw", image=matched_image_tk, tags="matched")
        self.canvas_frame.image_matched = matched_image_tk

        # Update scroll region
        self.canvas_frame.config(scrollregion=self.canvas_frame.bbox("all"))
```

ENTRY POINT

```python
if __name__ == "__main__":
    root = Tk()
    app = FASTMatcherApp(root)
    root.mainloop()
```

RUNNING PROGRAM

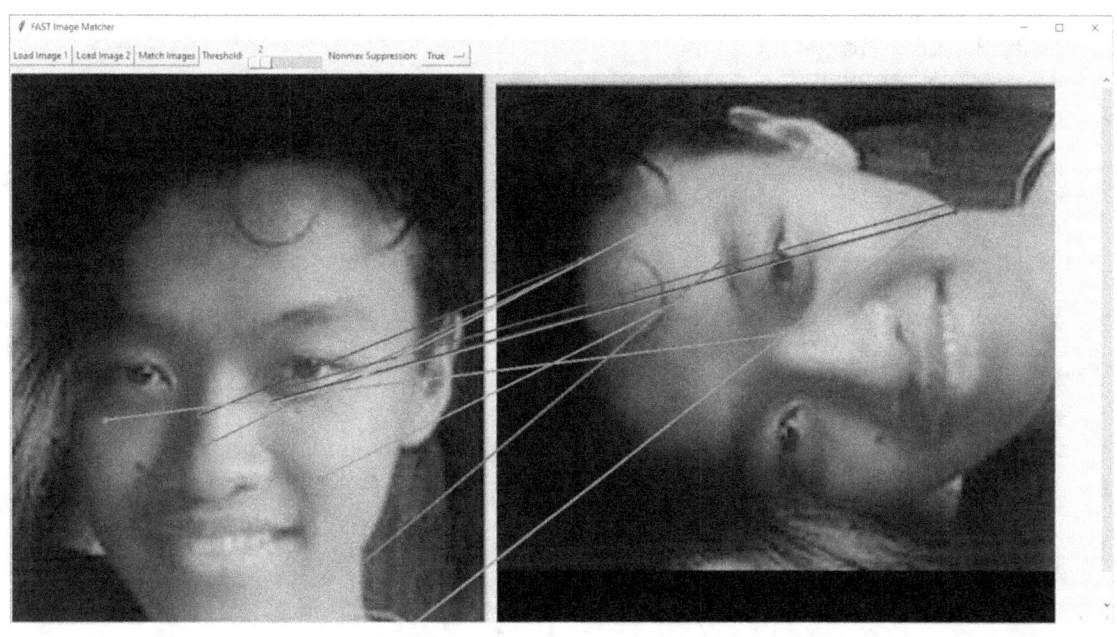

SOURCE CODE

```python
#FASTMatcher.py
import cv2
import numpy as np
from tkinter import Tk, Label, Button, filedialog, Canvas, Scale, Entry, StringVar, OptionMenu, HORIZONTAL, Scrollbar, RIGHT, BOTTOM, LEFT, Y, X
from PIL import Image, ImageTk

class FASTMatcherApp:
    def __init__(self, root):
        self.root = root
        self.root.title("FAST Image Matcher")

        # Frame for control widgets
        control_frame = Canvas(root)
        control_frame.pack(side="top", fill="x")

        self.load_button1 = Button(control_frame, text="Load Image 1", command=self.load_image1)
        self.load_button1.pack(side="left")

        self.load_button2 = Button(control_frame, text="Load Image 2", command=self.load_image2)
        self.load_button2.pack(side="left")

        self.match_button = Button(control_frame, text="Match Images", command=self.match_images)
        self.match_button.pack(side="left")

        # Parameters for FAST
        Label(control_frame, text="Threshold:").pack(side="left")
        self.threshold = Scale(control_frame, from_=0, to=255, orient=HORIZONTAL)
        self.threshold.pack(side="left")

        Label(control_frame, text="Nonmax Suppression:").pack(side="left")
        self.nonmaxSuppression = StringVar(root)
        self.nonmaxSuppression.set("True")
        OptionMenu(control_frame, self.nonmaxSuppression, "True", "False").pack(side="left")

        # Canvas with scrollbars
        self.canvas_frame = Canvas(root, width=1400, height=700)
        self.canvas_frame.pack(side="left", fill="both", expand=True)

        self.h_scrollbar = Scrollbar(root, orient="horizontal", command=self.canvas_frame.xview)
        self.h_scrollbar.pack(side=BOTTOM, fill=X)

        self.v_scrollbar = Scrollbar(root, orient="vertical", command=self.canvas_frame.yview)
        self.v_scrollbar.pack(side=RIGHT, fill=Y)

        self.canvas_frame.configure(xscrollcommand=self.h_scrollbar.set, yscrollcommand=self.v_scrollbar.set)
```

```python
        self.image1 = None
        self.image2 = None
        self.keypoints1 = None
        self.descriptors1 = None
        self.keypoints2 = None
        self.descriptors2 = None

    def load_image1(self):
        file_path = filedialog.askopenfilename()
        if file_path:
            self.image1 = cv2.imread(file_path)
            self.show_image(self.image1, 0, 0, 'image1')

    def load_image2(self):
        file_path = filedialog.askopenfilename()
        if file_path:
            self.image2 = cv2.imread(file_path)
            self.show_image(self.image2, 600, 0, 'image2')

    def show_image(self, image, x, y, tag):
        if len(image.shape) == 2:
            # If the image is grayscale
            image_rgb = cv2.cvtColor(image, cv2.COLOR_GRAY2RGB)
        else:
            # If the image is already in RGB
            image_rgb = cv2.cvtColor(image, cv2.COLOR_BGR2RGB)
        image_pil = Image.fromarray(image_rgb)
        image_tk = ImageTk.PhotoImage(image_pil)
        self.canvas_frame.create_image(x, y, anchor="nw", image=image_tk, tags=tag)
        setattr(self, f"{tag}_tk", image_tk)

        # Update scroll region
        self.canvas_frame.config(scrollregion=self.canvas_frame.bbox("all"))

    def match_images(self):
        if self.image1 is None or self.image2 is None:
            print("Please load both images first.")
            return

        # Get FAST parameters from user inputs
        threshold = self.threshold.get()
        nonmaxSuppression = True if self.nonmaxSuppression.get() == "True" else False

        # Initialize the FAST detector with user parameters
        fast        =        cv2.FastFeatureDetector_create(threshold=threshold, nonmaxSuppression=nonmaxSuppression)

        # Detect keypoints for both images
        keypoints1 = fast.detect(self.image1, None)
        keypoints2 = fast.detect(self.image2, None)

        # Compute descriptors for keypoints
        sift = cv2.SIFT_create()
        keypoints1, descriptors1 = sift.compute(self.image1, keypoints1)
        keypoints2, descriptors2 = sift.compute(self.image2, keypoints2)

        # Use BFMatcher to match descriptors
        bf = cv2.BFMatcher(cv2.NORM_L2, crossCheck=True)
```

```python
        matches = bf.match(descriptors1, descriptors2)

        # Sort matches by distance
        matches = sorted(matches, key=lambda x: x.distance)

        # Draw lines between matched keypoints
        matched_image = cv2.drawMatches(self.image1, keypoints1, self.image2, keypoints2, matches[:10], None, flags=cv2.DrawMatchesFlags_NOT_DRAW_SINGLE_POINTS)

        # Draw thicker lines manually
        for match in matches[:10]:
            img1_idx = match.queryIdx
            img2_idx = match.trainIdx
            (x1, y1) = keypoints1[img1_idx].pt
            (x2, y2) = keypoints2[img2_idx].pt
            x2 += self.image1.shape[1]  # Offset by width of image1 to account for combined image width

            # Use random color for the lines (same as drawMatches)
            color = tuple(np.random.randint(0, 255, 3).tolist())
            cv2.line(matched_image, (int(x1), int(y1)), (int(x2), int(y2)), color, 2)

        # Convert matched_image to RGB
        matched_image_rgb = cv2.cvtColor(matched_image, cv2.COLOR_BGR2RGB)
        matched_image_pil = Image.fromarray(matched_image_rgb)
        matched_image_tk = ImageTk.PhotoImage(matched_image_pil)

        # Clear the canvas before displaying the matched image
        self.canvas_frame.delete("image1")
        self.canvas_frame.delete("image2")

        # Display matched image
        self.canvas_frame.create_image(0, 0, anchor="nw", image=matched_image_tk, tags="matched")
        self.canvas_frame.image_matched = matched_image_tk

        # Update scroll region
        self.canvas_frame.config(scrollregion=self.canvas_frame.bbox("all"))

if __name__ == "__main__":
    root = Tk()
    app = FASTMatcherApp(root)
    root.mainloop()
```

AGAST IMAGE MATCHING

PURPOSE OF PROJECT

The AGASTMatcherApp class provides a graphical user interface (GUI) for matching keypoints between two images using the AGAST (Adaptive and Generic Accelerated Segment Test) algorithm. It leverages OpenCV for image processing and Tkinter for the GUI. Here's a detailed breakdown of the code:

First, the AGASTMatcherApp class initializes the main window, setting its title to "AGAST Image Matcher." It creates a frame, control_frame, to hold the control buttons and sliders for user interaction. This frame is packed at the top of the window and contains buttons for loading images, matching images, and adjusting parameters.

Next, two buttons, load_button1 and load_button2, are created and packed into the control frame. These buttons allow the user to load two separate images by invoking the load_image1() and load_image2() methods. Each method opens a file dialog for the user to select an image file, loads the image using OpenCV's cv2.imread(), and displays it on the canvas using the show_image() method.

The show_image() method handles the display of loaded images on the canvas. It checks if the image is grayscale and converts it to RGB if necessary. The image is then converted to a format compatible with Tkinter using the Python Imaging Library (PIL) and displayed on the canvas at specified coordinates. The canvas is also configured with scrollbars to handle large images, ensuring the entire image can be viewed by scrolling.

The control frame includes widgets to adjust parameters for the AGAST detector and the BRIEF descriptor. A scale widget allows the user to set the threshold for keypoint detection, while an option menu lets the user toggle non-maximum suppression. Additionally, an entry widget lets the user specify the number of bytes for the BRIEF descriptor, providing flexibility in how the descriptors are computed.

When the match_button is clicked, the match_images() method is invoked. This method first checks if both images have been loaded. If not, it prints a message asking the user to load both images. It then retrieves the AGAST parameters from the user inputs and initializes the AGAST detector with these parameters. The detector is used to find keypoints in both images.

After detecting the keypoints, the method retrieves the number of bytes for the BRIEF descriptor from the user input. It initializes the BRIEF descriptor and computes the descriptors for both images. To match the descriptors, it uses the BFMatcher with the Hamming distance, which is suitable for binary descriptors like those produced by BRIEF.

The matches are sorted by distance, and the top matches are drawn on the canvas. The cv2.drawMatches function is used to draw the matches, and thicker lines are manually added for better visualization. Each line is drawn between corresponding keypoints in the two images, using random colors to distinguish different matches.

Finally, the matched image is converted to RGB, then to a format compatible with Tkinter using PIL, and displayed on the canvas. The previous images are cleared from the canvas before displaying the matched image, ensuring a clean presentation. The canvas scroll region is updated to accommodate the new image size, allowing users to scroll through the entire matched image.

Overall, the AGASTMatcherApp class provides an interactive way to load, display, and match keypoints between two images using AGAST and BRIEF algorithms. The GUI elements facilitate user interaction, making it easy to adjust parameters and view the results.

MATCHING IMAGES

The match_images() method in the AGASTMatcherApp class is responsible for detecting and matching keypoints between two loaded images using the AGAST and BRIEF algorithms. Here's a detailed explanation of its purpose and functionality:

1. Image Loading Check: The method begins by checking if both images have been loaded. If either self.image1 or self.image2 is None, it prints a message prompting the user to load both images first. This ensures that the subsequent image processing steps have the necessary data to work with.
2. AGAST Parameters: The method retrieves the AGAST parameters from user inputs. The threshold is obtained from a scale widget, and nonmaxSuppression is a boolean value derived from an option menu. These parameters are essential for configuring the AGAST detector.
3. AGAST Detector Initialization: Using the retrieved parameters, the AGAST detector is initialized with cv2.AgastFeatureDetector_create. This detector is used to find keypoints in both images. Keypoints are distinctive points in an image that can be used for matching.
4. Keypoint Detection: The detector's detect method is called on both images, storing the detected keypoints in self.keypoints1 and self.keypoints2. These keypoints are the areas of interest that the algorithm identifies based on the specified parameters.
5. BRIEF Parameters: The method retrieves the number of bytes for the BRIEF descriptor from a user input field. This value determines the size of the descriptor that will be computed for each keypoint.
6. BRIEF Descriptor Initialization: The BRIEF descriptor extractor is initialized using cv2.xfeatures2d.BriefDescriptorExtractor_create. This extractor will compute binary descriptors for each keypoint, which are compact representations used for matching.
7. Descriptor Computation: The method computes the BRIEF descriptors for the keypoints in both images using the brief.compute method. The computed descriptors are stored in self.descriptors1 and self.descriptors2.
8. Descriptor Matching: To match the descriptors between the two images, the method uses the BFMatcher with Hamming distance. The BFMatcher's match method is called to find the best matches between the descriptors. The matches are then sorted by distance, with shorter distances indicating better matches.
9. Drawing Matches: The top matches are drawn on a combined image using cv2.drawMatches. The method iterates through the matches, drawing lines between corresponding keypoints in the two images. These lines are drawn in random colors to visually distinguish different matches.

10. Displaying the Matched Image: The matched image, which shows both images side by side with lines connecting matched keypoints, is converted to RGB format and then to a format compatible with Tkinter using PIL. The canvas is cleared of the original images, and the matched image is displayed. The canvas's scroll region is updated to accommodate the new image size, allowing users to scroll through the entire matched image.

In summary, the match_images() method automates the process of detecting and matching keypoints between two images. It uses the AGAST algorithm for keypoint detection and the BRIEF descriptor for computing descriptors. The matched keypoints are then visually represented on the canvas, providing a clear and interactive way for users to see the similarities between the two images.

RUNNING PROGRAM

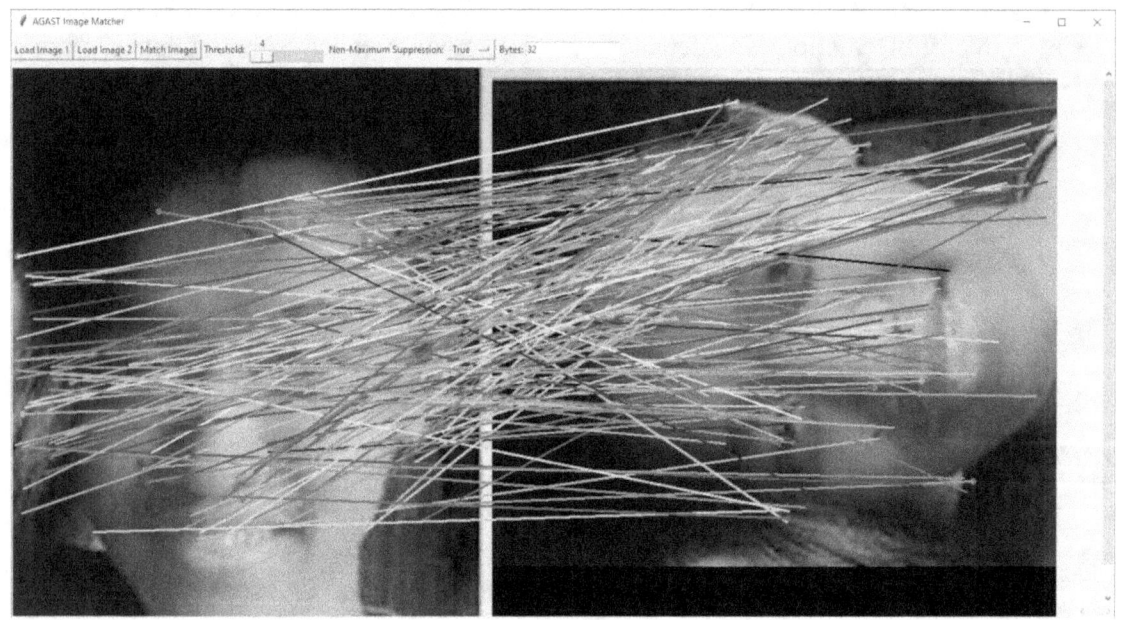

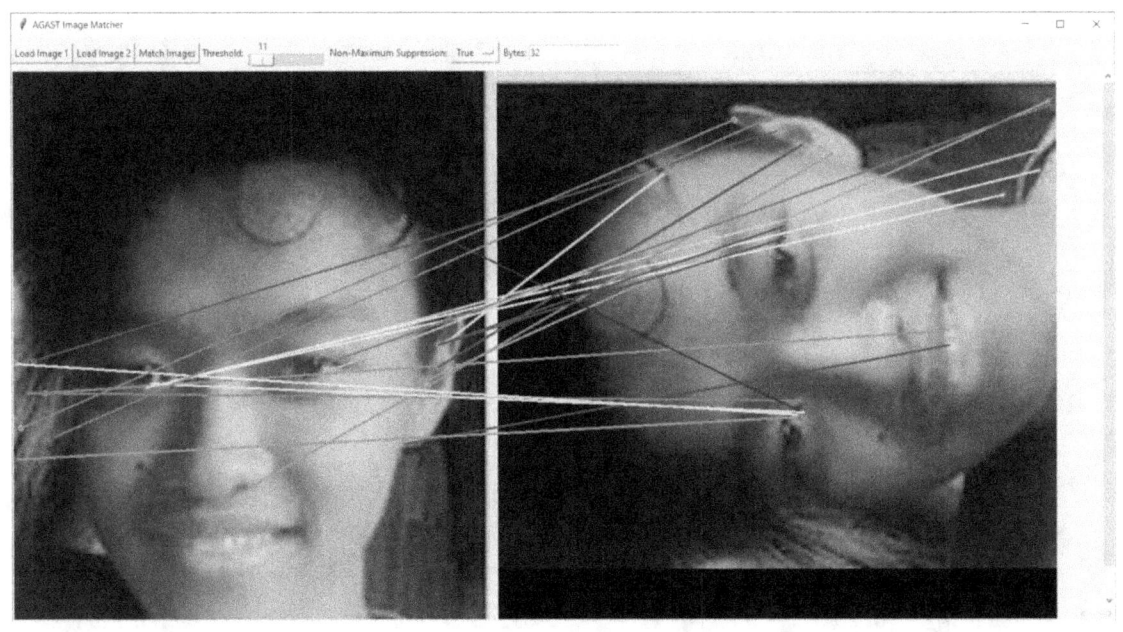

SOURCE CODE

```
#AGASTMatcher.py
import cv2
import numpy as np
from tkinter import Tk, Label, Button, filedialog, Canvas, Scale, Entry, StringVar,
OptionMenu, HORIZONTAL, Scrollbar, RIGHT, BOTTOM, LEFT, Y, X
from PIL import Image, ImageTk
from PIL import Image, ImageTk

class AGASTMatcherApp:
    def __init__(self, root):
        self.root = root
        self.root.title("AGAST Image Matcher")

        # Frame for control widgets
        control_frame = Canvas(root)
        control_frame.pack(side="top", fill="x")

        self.load_button1    =    Button(control_frame,    text="Load    Image    1",
command=self.load_image1)
        self.load_button1.pack(side="left")

        self.load_button2    =    Button(control_frame,    text="Load    Image    2",
command=self.load_image2)
        self.load_button2.pack(side="left")

        self.match_button    =    Button(control_frame,    text="Match    Images",
command=self.match_images)
        self.match_button.pack(side="left")
```

```python
        # Parameters for AGAST
        Label(control_frame, text="Threshold:").pack(side="left")
        self.threshold = Scale(control_frame, from_=1, to=255, orient=HORIZONTAL)
        self.threshold.pack(side="left")

        Label(control_frame, text="Non-Maximum Suppression:").pack(side="left")
        self.nonmaxSuppression = StringVar(control_frame)
        self.nonmaxSuppression.set("True")
        OptionMenu(control_frame, self.nonmaxSuppression, "True", "False").pack(side="left")

        # Parameters for AGAST
        Label(control_frame, text="Bytes:").pack(side="left")
        self.bytes = Entry(control_frame)
        self.bytes.insert(0, "32")
        self.bytes.pack(side="left")

        # Canvas with scrollbars
        self.canvas_frame = Canvas(root, width=1400, height=700)
        self.canvas_frame.pack(side="left", fill="both", expand=True)

        self.h_scrollbar = Scrollbar(root, orient="horizontal", command=self.canvas_frame.xview)
        self.h_scrollbar.pack(side=BOTTOM, fill=X)

        self.v_scrollbar = Scrollbar(root, orient="vertical", command=self.canvas_frame.yview)
        self.v_scrollbar.pack(side=RIGHT, fill=Y)

        self.canvas_frame.configure(xscrollcommand=self.h_scrollbar.set, yscrollcommand=self.v_scrollbar.set)

        self.image1 = None
        self.image2 = None
        self.keypoints1 = None
        self.descriptors1 = None
        self.keypoints2 = None
        self.descriptors2 = None

    def load_image1(self):
        file_path = filedialog.askopenfilename()
        if file_path:
            self.image1 = cv2.imread(file_path)
            self.show_image(self.image1, 0, 0, 'image1')

    def load_image2(self):
        file_path = filedialog.askopenfilename()
        if file_path:
            self.image2 = cv2.imread(file_path)
            self.show_image(self.image2, 600, 0, 'image2')

    def show_image(self, image, x, y, tag):
        if len(image.shape) == 2:
            # If the image is grayscale
            image_rgb = cv2.cvtColor(image, cv2.COLOR_GRAY2RGB)
        else:
            # If the image is already in RGB
```

```python
            image_rgb = cv2.cvtColor(image, cv2.COLOR_BGR2RGB)
        image_pil = Image.fromarray(image_rgb)
        image_tk = ImageTk.PhotoImage(image_pil)
        self.canvas_frame.create_image(x, y, anchor="nw", image=image_tk, tags=tag)
        setattr(self, f"{tag}_tk", image_tk)

        # Update scroll region
        self.canvas_frame.config(scrollregion=self.canvas_frame.bbox("all"))

    def match_images(self):
        if self.image1 is None or self.image2 is None:
            print("Please load both images first.")
            return

        # Get AGAST parameters from user inputs
        threshold = self.threshold.get()
        nonmaxSuppression = self.nonmaxSuppression.get() == "True"

        # Initialize the AGAST detector with user parameters
        detector         =         cv2.AgastFeatureDetector_create(threshold=threshold, nonmaxSuppression=nonmaxSuppression)

        # Detect keypoints and compute descriptors for both images
        self.keypoints1 = detector.detect(self.image1)
        self.keypoints2 = detector.detect(self.image2)

        # Get BRIEF parameters from user inputs
        bytes_ = int(self.bytes.get())

        # Initialize the BRIEF descriptor
        brief = cv2.xfeatures2d.BriefDescriptorExtractor_create(bytes=bytes_)

        # Compute descriptors for both images
        _, self.descriptors1 = brief.compute(self.image1, self.keypoints1)
        _, self.descriptors2 = brief.compute(self.image2, self.keypoints2)

        # Use BFMatcher to match descriptors with user parameters
        bf = cv2.BFMatcher(cv2.NORM_HAMMING, crossCheck=True)
        matches = bf.match(self.descriptors1, self.descriptors2)

        # Sort matches by distance
        matches = sorted(matches, key=lambda x: x.distance)

        # Draw top matches
        matched_image    =   cv2.drawMatches(self.image1,   self.keypoints1,  self.image2, self.keypoints2,                         matches[:50],                             None, flags=cv2.DrawMatchesFlags_NOT_DRAW_SINGLE_POINTS)

        # Draw thicker lines manually
        for match in matches:
            img1_idx = match.queryIdx
            img2_idx = match.trainIdx
            (x1, y1) = self.keypoints1[img1_idx].pt
            (x2, y2) = self.keypoints2[img2_idx].pt
            x2 += self.image1.shape[1]  # Offset by width of image1 to account for combined image width

            # Use random color for the lines (same as drawMatches)
```

```python
            color = tuple(np.random.randint(0, 255, 3).tolist())
            cv2.line(matched_image, (int(x1), int(y1)), (int(x2), int(y2)), color, 2)

        # Convert matched_image to RGB
        matched_image_rgb = cv2.cvtColor(matched_image, cv2.COLOR_BGR2RGB)
        matched_image_pil = Image.fromarray(matched_image_rgb)
        matched_image_tk = ImageTk.PhotoImage(matched_image_pil)

        # Clear the canvas before displaying the matched image
        self.canvas_frame.delete("image1")
        self.canvas_frame.delete("image2")

        # Display matched image
        self.canvas_frame.create_image(0,   0,  anchor="nw",  image=matched_image_tk, tags="matched")
        self.canvas_frame.image_matched = matched_image_tk

if __name__ == "__main__":
    root = Tk()
    app = AGASTMatcherApp(root)
    root.mainloop()
```

AKAZE IMAGE MATCHING

PURPOSE OF PROJECT

The AKAZEMatcherApp project is a Python-based application designed to load, process, and match keypoints between two images using the AKAZE feature detection algorithm. The application is built using the OpenCV library for image processing and Tkinter for the graphical user interface (GUI).

The application starts with the initialization of the main window using Tkinter, setting the title to "AKAZE Image Matcher". The main interface includes buttons for loading two images and a button to initiate the matching process. Additionally, there are controls for adjusting the AKAZE parameters, such as the detection threshold, number of octaves, and number of octave layers, allowing users to fine-tune the feature detection process.

When the user clicks the button to load an image, a file dialog opens to select an image file. The selected image is then read using OpenCV, converted to a format suitable for display with Tkinter, and displayed on a canvas. The canvas is equipped with scrollbars to navigate large images easily.

The core functionality of the application lies in the match_images method. This method first checks if both images are loaded; if not, it prompts the user to load the images. It then retrieves the user-specified AKAZE parameters and initializes the AKAZE detector with these settings. The AKAZE detector is used to detect keypoints and compute descriptors for each image.

To match the detected keypoints, the application uses the BFMatcher with Hamming distance. This matcher finds the best matches between the descriptors from the two images. The matches are sorted based on their distance, with the closest matches indicating higher similarity.

The application visualizes the matches by drawing lines between corresponding keypoints in the two images. These lines are color-coded randomly for better distinction. The matched image, combining both input images side by side with the matching lines, is then displayed on the canvas.

The application also ensures that the canvas is cleared before displaying the new matched image to avoid any overlaps or residual images from previous operations. The scroll region of the canvas is updated to accommodate the size of the new matched image, providing a smooth and intuitive user experience.

Overall, the AKAZEMatcherApp provides a user-friendly interface for image matching using the AKAZE algorithm. It allows users to load images, adjust detection parameters, and visualize the matching keypoints, making it a powerful tool for image analysis and comparison. This project showcases the integration of advanced image processing techniques with a simple yet effective GUI, highlighting the potential of Python and its libraries in developing practical applications.

MATCHING IMAGES

The match_images method in the AKAZEMatcherApp class is crucial for performing image matching using the AKAZE feature detection and description algorithm. Let's break down the functionality and purpose of this method in detail:
1. Input Image Validation: The method begins with a check to ensure that both image1 and image2 have been loaded. If either image is missing, it prints a message prompting the user to load both images before proceeding further. This validation ensures that the matching process operates on valid input data.
2. Retrieve AKAZE Parameters: After validating the input images, the method retrieves the AKAZE algorithm parameters set by the user through the GUI controls. These parameters include:

- threshold: Controls the feature detection sensitivity.
- nOctaves: Specifies the number of octaves to detect keypoints across different scales.
- nOctaveLayers: Determines the number of layers within each octave used in the feature detection process.

3. AKAZE Initialization: Using the retrieved parameters, the method initializes the AKAZE detector (akaze) using cv2.AKAZE_create(). This sets up the detector with the specified feature detection parameters (threshold, nOctaves, nOctaveLayers).

4. Detect and Compute Keypoints and Descriptors: The AKAZE detector (akaze) is then used to detect keypoints (keypoints1, keypoints2) and compute descriptors (descriptors1, descriptors2) for both image1 and image2. This step identifies distinctive points in each image and computes numerical representations (descriptors) that characterize these points.

5. Match Descriptors Using BFMatcher: Next, a Brute-Force Matcher (bf) is created with cv2.BFMatcher using Hamming distance (cv2.NORM_HAMMING) and setting crossCheck=True. This matcher compares descriptors from image1 (descriptors1) with those from image2 (descriptors2) to find the best matches between corresponding keypoints in both images.

6. Sort Matches: The resulting matches are sorted based on their distance, where a smaller distance indicates a closer match between descriptors.

7. Visualize Matches: To visualize the matched keypoints between image1 and image2, the method uses cv2.drawMatches to draw lines between the corresponding keypoints found in both images. It restricts visualization to the top 50 matches (matches[:50]) and ensures that single keypoints are not individually marked (cv2.DrawMatchesFlags_NOT_DRAW_SINGLE_POINTS).

8. Enhance Visualization: After drawing the initial matches, thicker lines are manually drawn between the keypoints using random colors. This enhances the visibility and distinction of matched keypoints on the displayed image (matched_image).

9. Display Matched Image: The final matched image (matched_image_tk), which incorporates both input images side by side with matching lines, is converted to RGB format (cv2.cvtColor(matched_image, cv2.COLOR_BGR2RGB)) and then transformed into a Tkinter-compatible format (ImageTk.PhotoImage). It replaces any existing images (image1, image2) on the canvas (canvas_frame) tagged as "image1" or "image2" with the newly created matched image. The canvas is

updated to display this matched image (canvas_frame.create_image) and retains a reference to it (canvas_frame.image_matched).
10. Update Scroll Region: Finally, the scroll region of the canvas (canvas_frame) is adjusted to encompass the entire displayed content using self.canvas_frame.config(scrollregion=self.canvas_frame.bbox("all")). This ensures that users can navigate through the entire matched image comfortably using the scrollbar controls provided.

In summary, the match_images() method orchestrates the entire process of AKAZE feature detection, descriptor computation, matching, visualization, and display within a Tkinter-based GUI application. It exemplifies the integration of advanced computer vision techniques with user-friendly interface elements, providing a robust tool for visualizing and comparing keypoints across images.

RUNNING PROGRAM

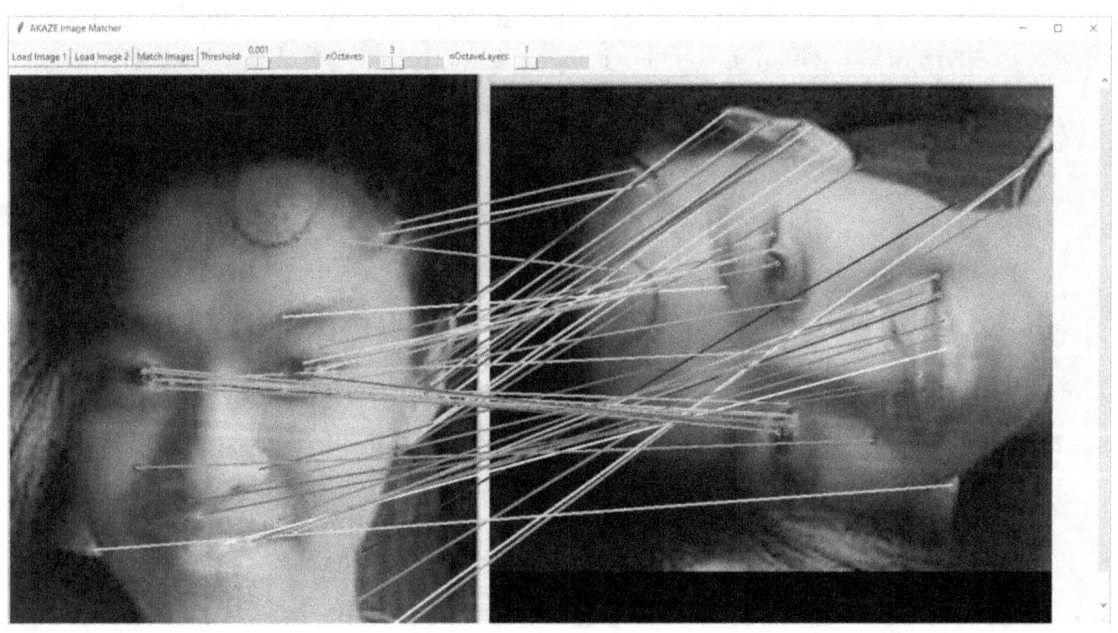

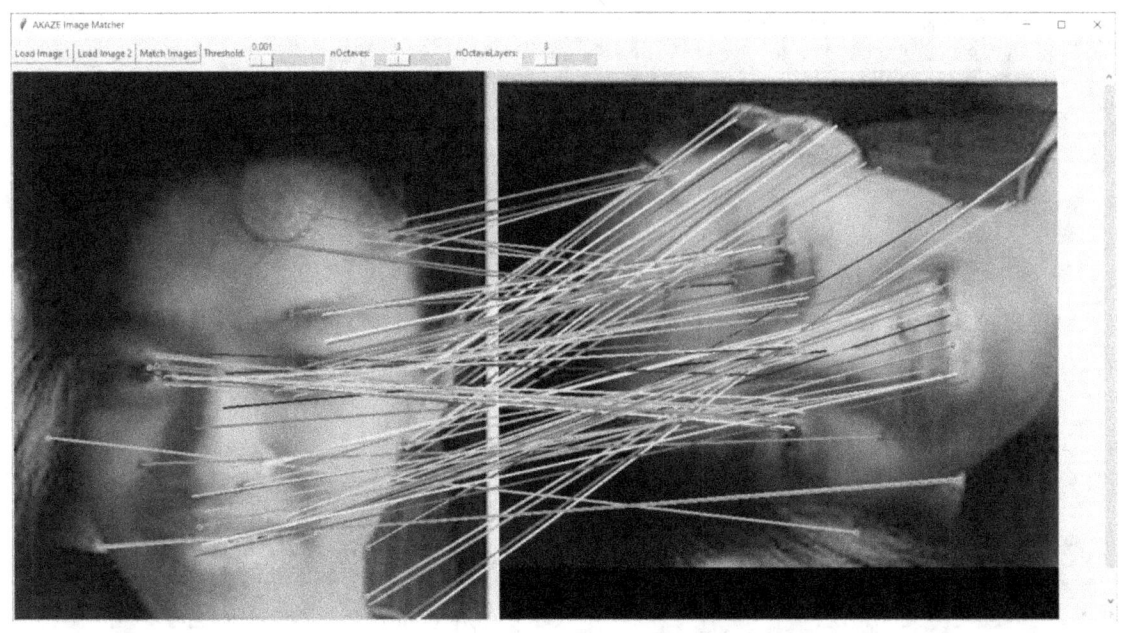

SOURCE CODE

```
#AKAZEMatcher.py
import cv2
import numpy as np
from tkinter import Tk, Label, Button, filedialog, Canvas, Scale, StringVar, OptionMenu, HORIZONTAL, Scrollbar, RIGHT, BOTTOM, Y, X
from PIL import Image, ImageTk

class AKAZEMatcherApp:
    def __init__(self, root):
        self.root = root
        self.root.title("AKAZE Image Matcher")

        # Frame for control widgets
        control_frame = Canvas(root)
        control_frame.pack(side="top", fill="x")

        self.load_button1 = Button(control_frame, text="Load Image 1", command=self.load_image1)
        self.load_button1.pack(side="left")

        self.load_button2 = Button(control_frame, text="Load Image 2", command=self.load_image2)
        self.load_button2.pack(side="left")

        self.match_button = Button(control_frame, text="Match Images", command=self.match_images)
        self.match_button.pack(side="left")
```

```python
        # Parameters for AKAZE
        Label(control_frame, text="Threshold:").pack(side="left")
        self.threshold = Scale(control_frame, from_=0.001, to=0.1, resolution=0.001, orient=HORIZONTAL)
        self.threshold.pack(side="left")

        Label(control_frame, text="nOctaves:").pack(side="left")
        self.nOctaves = Scale(control_frame, from_=1, to=10, orient=HORIZONTAL)
        self.nOctaves.pack(side="left")

        Label(control_frame, text="nOctaveLayers:").pack(side="left")
        self.nOctaveLayers = Scale(control_frame, from_=1, to=10, orient=HORIZONTAL)
        self.nOctaveLayers.pack(side="left")

        # Canvas with scrollbars
        self.canvas_frame = Canvas(root, width=1400, height=700)
        self.canvas_frame.pack(side="left", fill="both", expand=True)

        self.h_scrollbar = Scrollbar(root, orient="horizontal", command=self.canvas_frame.xview)
        self.h_scrollbar.pack(side=BOTTOM, fill=X)

        self.v_scrollbar = Scrollbar(root, orient="vertical", command=self.canvas_frame.yview)
        self.v_scrollbar.pack(side=RIGHT, fill=Y)

        self.canvas_frame.configure(xscrollcommand=self.h_scrollbar.set, yscrollcommand=self.v_scrollbar.set)

        self.image1 = None
        self.image2 = None
        self.keypoints1 = None
        self.descriptors1 = None
        self.keypoints2 = None
        self.descriptors2 = None

    def load_image1(self):
        file_path = filedialog.askopenfilename()
        if file_path:
            self.image1 = cv2.imread(file_path)
            self.show_image(self.image1, 0, 0, 'image1')

    def load_image2(self):
        file_path = filedialog.askopenfilename()
        if file_path:
            self.image2 = cv2.imread(file_path)
            self.show_image(self.image2, 600, 0, 'image2')

    def show_image(self, image, x, y, tag):
        if len(image.shape) == 2:
            # If the image is grayscale
            image_rgb = cv2.cvtColor(image, cv2.COLOR_GRAY2RGB)
        else:
            # If the image is already in RGB
            image_rgb = cv2.cvtColor(image, cv2.COLOR_BGR2RGB)
        image_pil = Image.fromarray(image_rgb)
        image_tk = ImageTk.PhotoImage(image_pil)
        self.canvas_frame.create_image(x, y, anchor="nw", image=image_tk, tags=tag)
```

```python
        setattr(self, f"{tag}_tk", image_tk)

        # Update scroll region
        self.canvas_frame.config(scrollregion=self.canvas_frame.bbox("all"))

    def match_images(self):
        if self.image1 is None or self.image2 is None:
            print("Please load both images first.")
            return

        # Get AKAZE parameters from user inputs
        threshold = self.threshold.get()
        nOctaves = self.nOctaves.get()
        nOctaveLayers = self.nOctaveLayers.get()

        # Initialize the AKAZE detector with user parameters
        akaze    =    cv2.AKAZE_create(threshold=threshold,    nOctaves=nOctaves,
nOctaveLayers=nOctaveLayers)

        # Detect keypoints and compute descriptors for both images
        self.keypoints1, self.descriptors1 = akaze.detectAndCompute(self.image1, None)
        self.keypoints2, self.descriptors2 = akaze.detectAndCompute(self.image2, None)

        # Use BFMatcher to match descriptors
        bf = cv2.BFMatcher(cv2.NORM_HAMMING, crossCheck=True)
        matches = bf.match(self.descriptors1, self.descriptors2)

        # Sort matches by distance
        matches = sorted(matches, key=lambda x: x.distance)

        # Draw top matches
        matched_image  =  cv2.drawMatches(self.image1,  self.keypoints1,  self.image2,
self.keypoints2,                         matches[:50],                          None,
flags=cv2.DrawMatchesFlags_NOT_DRAW_SINGLE_POINTS)

        # Draw thicker lines manually
        for match in matches:
            img1_idx = match.queryIdx
            img2_idx = match.trainIdx
            (x1, y1) = self.keypoints1[img1_idx].pt
            (x2, y2) = self.keypoints2[img2_idx].pt
            x2 += self.image1.shape[1]   # Offset by width of image1 to account for
combined image width

            # Use random color for the lines (same as drawMatches)
            color = tuple(np.random.randint(0, 255, 3).tolist())
            cv2.line(matched_image, (int(x1), int(y1)), (int(x2), int(y2)), color, 2)

        # Convert matched_image to RGB
        matched_image_rgb = cv2.cvtColor(matched_image, cv2.COLOR_BGR2RGB)
        matched_image_pil = Image.fromarray(matched_image_rgb)
        matched_image_tk = ImageTk.PhotoImage(matched_image_pil)

        # Clear the canvas before displaying the matched image
        self.canvas_frame.delete("image1")
        self.canvas_frame.delete("image2")

        # Display matched image
```

```
        self.canvas_frame.create_image(0, 0, anchor="nw", image=matched_image_tk, tags="matched")
        self.canvas_frame.image_matched = matched_image_tk

        # Update scroll region
        self.canvas_frame.config(scrollregion=self.canvas_frame.bbox("all"))

if __name__ == "__main__":
    root = Tk()
    app = AKAZEMatcherApp(root)
    root.mainloop()
```

BRISK IMAGE MATCHING

PURPOSE OF PROJECT

The BRISKMatcherApp class is a Python application designed with Tkinter to facilitate the matching and visualization of keypoint descriptors between two images using the BRISK feature detection and description algorithm. Let's break down its functionality into clear paragraphs:

1. Graphical Interface Setup: Upon initialization, the application creates a Tkinter window (root) titled "BRISK Image Matcher". A canvas (control_frame) is positioned at the top to house control widgets such as buttons and sliders for user interaction.

2. Control Widgets: Three buttons are added to control_frame: "Load Image 1", "Load Image 2", and "Match Images". These buttons enable users to load two images and initiate the matching process between them. Each button is linked to respective methods (load_image1, load_image2, match_images) for functionality.

3. BRISK Parameters: Below the buttons, sliders (Scale widgets) allow users to adjust the parameters crucial for the BRISK algorithm: Threshold, Octaves, and Pattern Scale. These parameters determine how keypoint descriptors are detected and matched between images.

4. Image Display Canvas: Another canvas (canvas_frame) is included to display the loaded images and the matched result. This canvas is configured with scrollbars (h_scrollbar and v_scrollbar) to navigate through images of varying sizes.

5. Image Loading: The load_image1 and load_image2 methods use a file dialog to prompt users to select image files from their system. Upon selection, the chosen images are loaded using OpenCV (cv2.imread(file_path)) and displayed on canvas_frame in RGB format using the show_image method.
6. Image Display Method (show_image): This method converts images to RGB format if necessary and then to ImageTk.PhotoImage format compatible with Tkinter for display. It places the images on canvas_frame at specified coordinates (x, y) with unique tags ('image1' or 'image2'), ensuring they are visible within the defined scroll region.
7. Matching Process (match_images Method): This method handles the core functionality of the application. It checks if both images (image1 and image2) are loaded and prompts the user if they are not. Once both images are available, it retrieves the BRISK algorithm parameters set by the user and initializes the BRISK detector (brisk) accordingly.
8. Key Point Detection and Descriptor Calculation: Using the BRISK detector (brisk), the method detects keypoints (keypoints1, keypoints2) and computes descriptors (descriptors1, descriptors2) for both images. These descriptors encapsulate the unique features of each image that can be compared for matching.
9. Descriptor Matching: The application employs the Brute-Force Matcher (cv2.BFMatcher) to compare descriptors (descriptors1, descriptors2) and determine matching keypoints between the images. These matches are then sorted based on their distances.
10. Visualization: Finally, the matched keypoints are visualized on canvas_frame using cv2.drawMatches. This method draws lines between matched keypoints, enhancing their visibility with random colors. The resulting image is converted back to RGB format and displayed on canvas_frame, replacing any previously displayed images. The scroll region of canvas_frame is updated to accommodate the newly displayed image, ensuring smooth navigation and interaction.

In essence, the BRISKMatcherApp class encapsulates a user-friendly interface for loading images, adjusting key algorithm parameters, performing feature matching using BRISK, and visualizing the results dynamically within a Tkinter-based GUI framework. This setup enables users to explore and analyze similarities between images based on their distinctive keypoints and descriptors effectively.

MATCHING IMAGES

The match_images() method in the BRISKMatcherApp class handles the core functionality of matching keypoints and visualizing the results between two loaded images using the BRISK algorithm and Tkinter for GUI display. Here's a detailed explanation of each part of the method:

1. Image Check: The method first checks if both image1 and image2 are loaded. If either image is missing, it prints a message prompting the user to load both images before proceeding further.
2. Parameter Retrieval: If both images are loaded, the method retrieves user-defined BRISK parameters from the GUI controls. These parameters include threshold, octaves, and pattern_scale which influence how keypoints are detected and descriptors computed by the BRISK algorithm.
3. BRISK Detector Initialization: Using the retrieved parameters, a BRISK detector (brisk) is instantiated using cv2.BRISK_create. This detector is configured with the user-defined threshold for keypoint detection sensitivity, octaves for scale levels, and pattern scale to adjust the size of the sampling pattern for descriptor computation.
4. Keypoint Detection and Descriptor Calculation: The BRISK detector (brisk) is then applied to both image1 and image2 to detect keypoints (keypoints1, keypoints2) and compute their corresponding descriptors (descriptors1, descriptors2). These descriptors capture the unique characteristics of keypoints that can be used for matching.
5. Descriptor Matching: A Brute-Force Matcher (bf) is initialized with cv2.BFMatcher using the Hamming distance as the similarity metric (cv2.NORM_HAMMING) and enabling cross-checking (crossCheck=True) to ensure robust matching. The matcher compares descriptors from image1 and image2 (descriptors1 and descriptors2).
6. Drawing Matches: Using cv2.drawMatches, the method creates matched_image, which visualizes the matches found between image1 and image2 based on their keypoints (keypoints1, keypoints2). The matches list determines which keypoints are linked, and flags=cv2.DrawMatchesFlags_NOT_DRAW_SINGLE_POINTS ensures only matched keypoints are connected.
7. Enhancing Visualization: To improve visibility, the method manually draws thicker lines between matched keypoints. It iterates through each match in matches, retrieves their coordinates ((x1, y1) for image1 and (x2, y2) for image2), and adjusts x2 to account for the width of image1, ensuring lines connect points across both images seamlessly.

8. Coloring Lines: Each line connecting matched keypoints is colored with a randomly generated RGB color using NumPy (np.random.randint). This adds visual distinction to each match line.
9. Conversion and Display: The matched_image is converted from BGR to RGB format (cv2.cvtColor) to align with Tkinter's image display requirements (Image.fromarray). It's then converted to ImageTk.PhotoImage (ImageTk.PhotoImage(matched_image_pil)) for display on the Tkinter canvas (canvas_frame).
10. Canvas Update: Before displaying the matched image, any previous images ("image1" and "image2") are cleared from canvas_frame. The newly generated matched_image_tk is then displayed at coordinates (0, 0) with anchor "nw" (top-left corner), tagged as "matched". The scroll region of canvas_frame is updated to encompass the entire displayed image, ensuring smooth navigation within the canvas.

In summary, the match_images() method integrates image loading, BRISK feature detection and matching, custom line drawing for visual enhancement, and Tkinter-based GUI updates to facilitate intuitive exploration and comparison of keypoint-based similarities between two images.

RUNNING PROGRAM

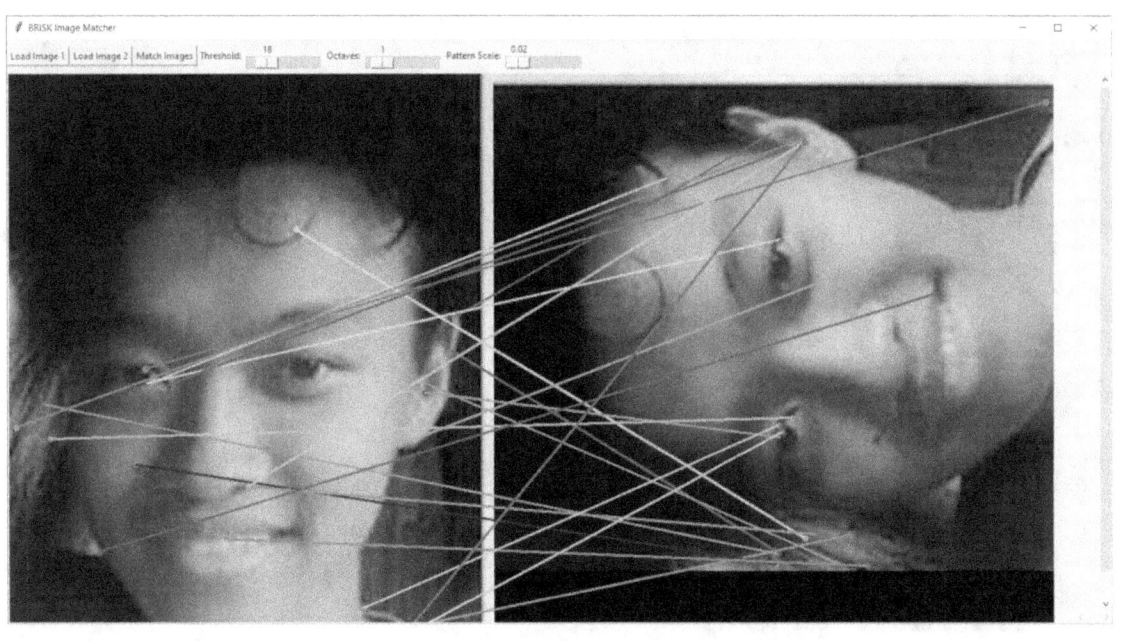

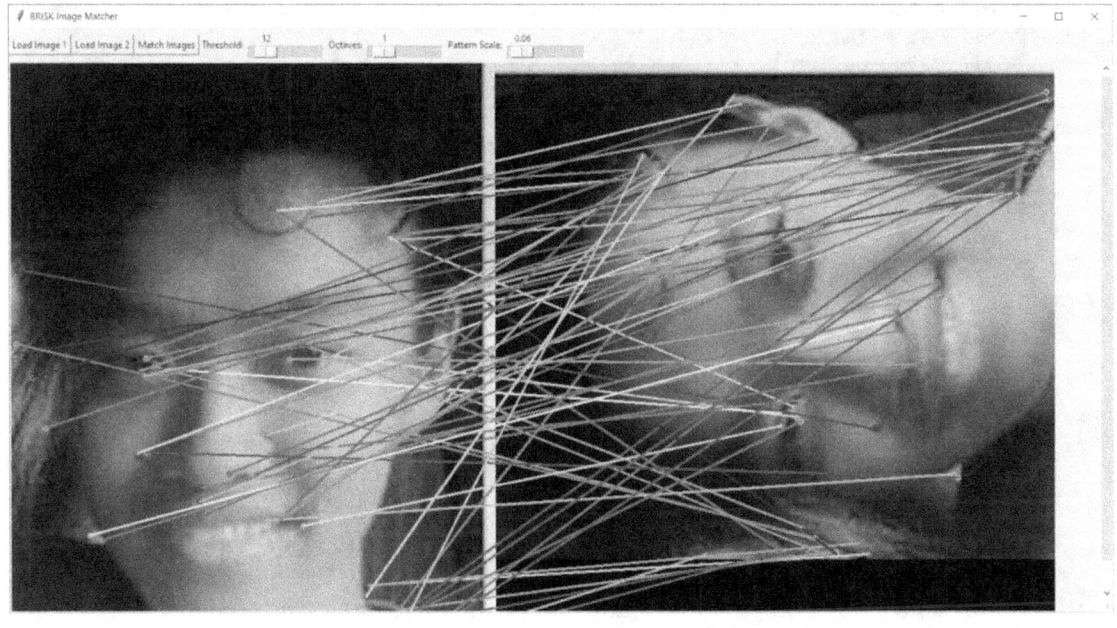

SOURCE CODE

```python
#BRISKMatcher.py
import cv2
import numpy as np
from tkinter import Tk, Label, Button, filedialog, Canvas, Scale, Entry, StringVar, OptionMenu, HORIZONTAL, Scrollbar, RIGHT, BOTTOM, LEFT, Y, X
from PIL import Image, ImageTk

class BRISKMatcherApp:
    def __init__(self, root):
        self.root = root
        self.root.title("BRISK Image Matcher")

        # Frame for control widgets
        control_frame = Canvas(root)
        control_frame.pack(side="top", fill="x")

        self.load_button1 = Button(control_frame, text="Load Image 1", command=self.load_image1)
        self.load_button1.pack(side="left")

        self.load_button2 = Button(control_frame, text="Load Image 2", command=self.load_image2)
        self.load_button2.pack(side="left")

        self.match_button = Button(control_frame, text="Match Images", command=self.match_images)
        self.match_button.pack(side="left")

        # Parameters for BRISK
        Label(control_frame, text="Threshold:").pack(side="left")
        self.threshold = Scale(control_frame, from_=0, to=100, orient=HORIZONTAL)
        self.threshold.pack(side="left")

        Label(control_frame, text="Octaves:").pack(side="left")
        self.octaves = Scale(control_frame, from_=0, to=10, orient=HORIZONTAL)
        self.octaves.pack(side="left")

        Label(control_frame, text="Pattern Scale:").pack(side="left")
        self.pattern_scale = Scale(control_frame, from_=0, to=1, resolution=0.01, orient=HORIZONTAL)
        self.pattern_scale.pack(side="left")

        # Canvas with scrollbars
        self.canvas_frame = Canvas(root, width=1400, height=700)
        self.canvas_frame.pack(side="left", fill="both", expand=True)

        self.h_scrollbar = Scrollbar(root, orient="horizontal", command=self.canvas_frame.xview)
        self.h_scrollbar.pack(side=BOTTOM, fill=X)

        self.v_scrollbar = Scrollbar(root, orient="vertical", command=self.canvas_frame.yview)
        self.v_scrollbar.pack(side=RIGHT, fill=Y)
```

```python
        self.canvas_frame.configure(xscrollcommand=self.h_scrollbar.set, 
yscrollcommand=self.v_scrollbar.set)

        self.image1 = None
        self.image2 = None
        self.keypoints1 = None
        self.descriptors1 = None
        self.keypoints2 = None
        self.descriptors2 = None

    def load_image1(self):
        file_path = filedialog.askopenfilename()
        if file_path:
            self.image1 = cv2.imread(file_path)
            self.show_image(self.image1, 0, 0, 'image1')

    def load_image2(self):
        file_path = filedialog.askopenfilename()
        if file_path:
            self.image2 = cv2.imread(file_path)
            self.show_image(self.image2, 600, 0, 'image2')

    def show_image(self, image, x, y, tag):
        if len(image.shape) == 2:
            # If the image is grayscale
            image_rgb = cv2.cvtColor(image, cv2.COLOR_GRAY2RGB)
        else:
            # If the image is already in RGB
            image_rgb = cv2.cvtColor(image, cv2.COLOR_BGR2RGB)
        image_pil = Image.fromarray(image_rgb)
        image_tk = ImageTk.PhotoImage(image_pil)
        self.canvas_frame.create_image(x, y, anchor="nw", image=image_tk, tags=tag)
        setattr(self, f"{tag}_tk", image_tk)

        # Update scroll region
        self.canvas_frame.config(scrollregion=self.canvas_frame.bbox("all"))

    def match_images(self):
        if self.image1 is None or self.image2 is None:
            print("Please load both images first.")
            return

        # Get BRISK parameters from user inputs
        threshold = self.threshold.get()
        octaves = self.octaves.get()
        pattern_scale = self.pattern_scale.get()

        # Initialize the BRISK detector with user parameters
        brisk      =      cv2.BRISK_create(thresh=threshold,       octaves=octaves, 
patternScale=pattern_scale)

        # Detect keypoints and compute descriptors for both images
        self.keypoints1, self.descriptors1 = brisk.detectAndCompute(self.image1, None)
        self.keypoints2, self.descriptors2 = brisk.detectAndCompute(self.image2, None)

        # Use BFMatcher to match descriptors
        bf = cv2.BFMatcher(cv2.NORM_HAMMING, crossCheck=True)
        matches = bf.match(self.descriptors1, self.descriptors2)
```

```python
        # Draw matches
        matched_image = cv2.drawMatches(self.image1, self.keypoints1, self.image2, self.keypoints2, matches, None, flags=cv2.DrawMatchesFlags_NOT_DRAW_SINGLE_POINTS)

        # Draw thicker lines manually
        for match in matches:
            img1_idx = match.queryIdx
            img2_idx = match.trainIdx
            (x1, y1) = self.keypoints1[img1_idx].pt
            (x2, y2) = self.keypoints2[img2_idx].pt
            x2 += self.image1.shape[1]  # Offset by width of image1 to account for combined image width

            # Use random color for the lines (same as drawMatches)
            color = tuple(np.random.randint(0, 255, 3).tolist())
            cv2.line(matched_image, (int(x1), int(y1)), (int(x2), int(y2)), color, 2)

        # Convert matched_image to RGB
        matched_image_rgb = cv2.cvtColor(matched_image, cv2.COLOR_BGR2RGB)
        matched_image_pil = Image.fromarray(matched_image_rgb)
        matched_image_tk = ImageTk.PhotoImage(matched_image_pil)

        # Clear the canvas before displaying the matched image
        self.canvas_frame.delete("image1")
        self.canvas_frame.delete("image2")

        # Display matched image
        self.canvas_frame.create_image(0, 0, anchor="nw", image=matched_image_tk, tags="matched")
        self.canvas_frame.image_matched = matched_image_tk

        # Update scroll region
        self.canvas_frame.config(scrollregion=self.canvas_frame.bbox("all"))

if __name__ == "__main__":
    root = Tk()
    app = BRISKMatcherApp(root)
    root.mainloop()
```

MATCHING CROPPED OBJECT IN VIDEO

PURPOSE OF PROJECT

The Python script (rgb_cropped_filtered_frame_object_matching.py) is designed to create a graphical user interface (GUI) application using the Tkinter library, facilitating the processing and analysis of video frames. Let's break down its functionality into simpler terms.

Firstly, the script begins by importing necessary libraries and modules such as Tkinter for building the GUI, Pillow (PIL) for image handling, imageio for video operations, OpenCV (cv2) for computer vision tasks, numpy for numerical computations, matplotlib for plotting, pywt for wavelet transforms, and os for system-level interactions.

The core of the script revolves around a class named Filter_CroppedFrame, which encapsulates the entire application. This class is initialized with a master parameter, representing the main window of the GUI. It sets the title of the window to "Object Matching Video" and initializes various attributes like file_name (to store the video file path), zoom_scale (to manage the zoom level of the video display), and others related to video playback and frame processing.

The create_widgets() method within the class configures and lays out all the graphical components of the application. These include control buttons (open_button, play_button, stop_button, prev_frame_button, next_frame_button) for video playback, comboboxes (zoom_combobox, filter_combobox, matcher_combobox) for selecting zoom levels, filters, and matchers respectively. Labels (frame_number_label, matcher_label) provide visual cues to the user about the current frame number and selected options.

For displaying the video, the application utilizes a canvas (canvas) within a video_panel. This canvas is where frames from the video are displayed. It supports interactions such as mouse scrolling (<MouseWheel> event), clicking (<ButtonPress-1>), dragging (<B1-Motion>), and releasing (<ButtonRelease-1>) for navigating through frames or interacting with specific regions of interest.

To facilitate video navigation and control, the application includes event handlers (open_video, toggle_play_pause, stop_video, prev_frame, next_frame) that respond to user actions triggered by the control buttons. These handlers manage tasks like opening a video file, starting or pausing video playback, stopping video playback, and navigating between frames.

Additionally, the script offers options for applying various image processing filters (filters list) and feature matching algorithms (matchers list) to the video frames. Users can select these options via comboboxes (filter_combobox, matcher_combobox) in the GUI. Selections trigger corresponding actions like applying filters or changing feature matching algorithms.

Lastly, the script includes scrollbars (scrollbar_vertical, scrollbar_horizontal) to allow scrolling through video frames vertically and horizontally when the canvas display exceeds its visible dimensions.

Overall, the script provides a comprehensive GUI application using Tkinter for interacting with video files, displaying frames, applying filters, and analyzing features through a user-friendly interface with responsive controls and interactive functionalities.

CLASS AND CONSTRUCTOR

The script initiates the creation of a graphical user interface (GUI) application using the Tkinter library. Let's explore how it sets up the application and its components:

Firstly, the script begins by importing necessary modules and libraries. Tkinter (tk) is imported as the core GUI toolkit, ttk for themed widgets, and filedialog for file operations within the GUI. From the PIL library, Image and ImageTk are imported for image manipulation and display in Tkinter. Additional libraries imported include imageio for video handling, pywt for wavelet transforms, cv2 for computer vision tasks, numpy for numerical operations, matplotlib.pyplot for plotting, subprocess for system-level operations, and os for general operating system functionalities.

The main class defined is Filter_CroppedFrame, which encapsulates the entire GUI application. It is initialized with a master parameter representing the main Tkinter window (self.master). The constructor (__init__ method) of this class performs several setup tasks:

- Window Configuration: Sets the title of the GUI window to "Object Matching Video".
- GUI Elements Initialization: Initializes several instance variables including file_name (to store the path of the currently opened video file), frame_number_label (a Tkinter Label widget to display the current frame number), video and video_path (to handle video data and its path), paused (to manage the video playback state), zoom_scale (an integer variable for zoom level control), frame_index (to track the current frame index), bbox (possibly for storing bounding box data related to object detection), and bbox_rect (initialized to None, likely for handling graphical bounding box representations).
- Filter and Matcher Lists: Defines lists (filters and matchers) containing strings representing various image processing filters and feature matching algorithms respectively. These lists will be used to populate comboboxes or provide options for the user to select specific filters and matchers.
- Widget Creation: Calls self.create_widgets() method to initialize and layout all GUI components. This includes buttons (open_button, play_button, stop_button, etc.) for video control, comboboxes (zoom_combobox, filter_combobox, matcher_combobox) for selecting zoom levels, filters, and matchers, and labels (frame_number_label) for displaying information to the user.

In summary, the script sets up a Tkinter-based GUI application (Filter_CroppedFrame) for video processing and analysis. It provides functionalities for opening video files, navigating frames, applying various image filters, selecting feature matching algorithms, and displaying video frames and processed images within a user-friendly interface. The use of Tkinter along with other imported libraries facilitates interactive control and visualization of video and image data in Python.

```
#rgb_cropped_filtered_frame_object__matching.py
import tkinter as tk
from tkinter import ttk
from tkinter import filedialog
from PIL import Image, ImageTk
import imageio
import pywt
import cv2
import numpy as np
import matplotlib.pyplot as plt
import subprocess
import os

class Filter_CroppedFrame:
    def __init__(self, master):
        self.master = master
        self.master.title("Object Matching Video")
        self.file_name = ""
        self.set_window_title()  # Set window title initially

        self.frame_number_label = tk.Label(master, text="Frame: 0")
        self.frame_number_label.pack()

        self.video = None
        self.video_path = None
        self.paused = False
        self.zoom_scale = tk.IntVar(value=1)
        self.frame_index = 0
        self.bbox = None
        self.bbox_rect = None  # Initialize bbox_rect attribute to None

        # Available filters
        self.filters = ["None", "Gaussian", "Mean", "Median", "Bilateral Filtering",
                    "Non-local Means Denoising", "Anisotropic Diffusion",
                    "Total Variation Denoising", "Wiener Filter",
                    "Adaptive Thresholding", "Haar Wavelet Transform",
                    "Daubechies Wavelet Transform", "SRCNN Super Resolution",
                    "EDSR Super Resolution"]

        # Available matchers
        self.matchers = ["SIFT", "ORB", "FAST", "AGAST", "BRISK", "AKAZE"]

        self.create_widgets()
```

CREATING WIDGETS

The create_widgets() method within the Filter_CroppedFrame class is responsible for setting up and arranging all the graphical user interface (GUI) elements that make up the application. Let's break down each section of this method and understand its purpose:

1. Control Panel Setup:
   - control_panel: This is a frame (tk.Frame) that contains control buttons and other interactive elements for video playback and navigation.
   - Configuration (padx=10, pady=(0, 10), fill="x"): Sets padding around the panel, with extra space at the bottom, and fills horizontally.
2. Open Video Button:
   - open_button: A tk.Button widget labeled "Open Video" that triggers the open_video method when clicked (command=self.open_video).
   - Placed in control_panel at row 0, column 0 with padding (padx=10, pady=5).
3. Zoom Combobox:
   - zoom_combobox: A ttk.Combobox widget for selecting zoom levels (values=list(range(1, 11))).
   - Displays current zoom level (textvariable=self.zoom_scale) and triggers update_zoom method on selection (<<ComboboxSelected>> event).
   - Positioned in control_panel at row 0, column 1 with padding.
4. Play/Pause Button:
   - play_button: A tk.Button labeled "Play/Pause" that toggles video playback (command=self.toggle_play_pause).
   - Located in control_panel at row 0, column 2 with padding.
5. Stop Button:
   - stop_button: A tk.Button labeled "Stop" that halts video playback (command=self.stop_video).
   - Placed in control_panel at row 0, column 3 with padding.
6. Frame Navigation Buttons:
   - prev_frame_button and next_frame_button: tk.Button widgets labeled "Previous Frame" and "Next Frame".
   - They trigger prev_frame and next_frame methods respectively for navigating through video frames.
   - Positioned in control_panel at columns 4 and 5 with padding.
7. Open New Instance Button:

- open_new_instance_button: A tk.Button labeled "Open New Instance" that initiates a new instance of the application (command=self.open_new_instance).
- Placed in control_panel at row 0, column 6 with padding.

8. Filter and Matcher Selection:
    - matcher_label and filter_label: tk.Label widgets for displaying text labels "Select Filter:" and "Select Matcher:".
    - Positioned in control_panel at columns 7 and 9 respectively, with sticky alignment to the east (sticky="e").

9. Comboboxes for Filters and Matchers:
    - filter_combobox and matcher_combobox: ttk.Combobox widgets populated with options from self.filters and self.matchers lists.
    - Default selections set to the first item (current(0)).
    - matcher_combobox triggers choose_matcher method on selection (<<ComboboxSelected>> event).
    - Positioned in control_panel at columns 8 and 10 with appropriate padding.

10. Video Panel Setup:
    - video_panel: Another frame (tk.Frame) where the video canvas (self.canvas) and scrollbars are placed.
    - Padding (padx=10, pady=10) ensures space around the video display area.

11. Canvas for Video Display:
    - self.canvas: A tk.Canvas widget used to display video frames with dimensions canvas_width and canvas_height.
    - Configured to expand (expand=True) and fill the available space (fill="both") within video_panel.
    - Various events (<MouseWheel>, <ButtonPress-1>, <B1-Motion>, <ButtonRelease-1>) are bound to methods (on_mousewheel, on_press, on_drag, on_release) for handling user interactions like scrolling, clicking, dragging, and releasing on the canvas.

12. Scrollbars:
    - scrollbar_vertical and scrollbar_horizontal: tk.Scrollbar widgets attached to the canvas.
    - scrollbar_vertical controls vertical scrolling (orient="vertical") and is positioned on the right side of video_panel.
    - scrollbar_horizontal controls horizontal scrolling (orient="horizontal") and is placed at the bottom of the main window (self.master).

Overall, the create_widgets() method sets up a comprehensive GUI layout with buttons for video control, comboboxes for selecting filters and matchers, a canvas for displaying video frames with scrolling capabilities, and appropriate bindings for user interactions. This structure forms the foundation for a functional and interactive video processing application using Tkinter in Python.

```
def create_widgets(self):
    # Panel for control buttons
    control_panel = tk.Frame(self.master)
    control_panel.pack(padx=10, pady=(0, 10), fill="x")

    # Button to open a video file
    self.open_button = tk.Button(control_panel, text="Open Video", command=self.open_video)
    self.open_button.grid(row=0, column=0, padx=10, pady=5)

    # Combobox for selecting zoom scale
    self.zoom_combobox = ttk.Combobox(control_panel, textvariable=self.zoom_scale, values=list(range(1, 11)))
    self.zoom_combobox.grid(row=0, column=1, padx=10, pady=5)
    self.zoom_combobox.bind("<<ComboboxSelected>>", self.update_zoom)

    # Button to play/pause the video
    self.play_button = tk.Button(control_panel, text="Play/Pause", command=self.toggle_play_pause)
    self.play_button.grid(row=0, column=2, padx=10, pady=5)

    # Button to stop the video
    self.stop_button = tk.Button(control_panel, text="Stop", command=self.stop_video)
    self.stop_button.grid(row=0, column=3, padx=10, pady=5)

    # Button to navigate to the previous frame
    self.prev_frame_button = tk.Button(control_panel, text="Previous Frame", command=self.prev_frame)
    self.prev_frame_button.grid(row=0, column=4, padx=10, pady=5)

    # Button to navigate to the next frame
    self.next_frame_button = tk.Button(control_panel, text="Next Frame", command=self.next_frame)
    self.next_frame_button.grid(row=0, column=5, padx=10, pady=5)

    # Button to open new instance
    self.open_new_instance_button = tk.Button(control_panel, text="Open New Instance", command=self.open_new_instance)
    self.open_new_instance_button.grid(row=0, column=6, padx=10, pady=5)

    # Label for the selecting filters
    self.matcher_label = tk.Label(control_panel, text="Select Filter:")
    self.matcher_label.grid(row=0, column=7, padx=10, pady=5, sticky="e")

    # Combobox for selecting filters
    self.filter_combobox = ttk.Combobox(control_panel, values=self.filters)
    self.filter_combobox.grid(row=0, column=8, padx=10, pady=5)
```

```
        self.filter_combobox.current(0)  # Set default value

        # Label for the selecting matchers
        self.matcher_label = tk.Label(control_panel, text="Select Matcher:")
        self.matcher_label.grid(row=0, column=9, padx=10, pady=5, sticky="e")

        # Combobox for selecting matchers
        self.matcher_combobox = ttk.Combobox(control_panel, values=self.matchers)
        self.matcher_combobox.grid(row=0, column=10, padx=10, pady=5)
        self.matcher_combobox.current(0)  # Set default value
        self.matcher_combobox.bind("<<ComboboxSelected>>", lambda event: self.choose_matcher())

        # Panel for video display
        video_panel = tk.Frame(self.master)
        video_panel.pack(padx=10, pady=10)

        # Canvas to display the original video
        canvas_width = 1400
        canvas_height = 650
        self.canvas = tk.Canvas(video_panel, width=canvas_width, height=canvas_height)
        self.canvas.pack(side="left", fill="both", expand=True)
        self.canvas.bind("<MouseWheel>", self.on_mousewheel)
        self.canvas.bind("<ButtonPress-1>", self.on_press)
        self.canvas.bind("<B1-Motion>", self.on_drag)
        self.canvas.bind("<ButtonRelease-1>", self.on_release)  # Bind ButtonRelease event

        self.scrollbar_vertical = tk.Scrollbar(video_panel, orient="vertical", command=self.canvas.yview)
        self.scrollbar_vertical.pack(side="right", fill="y")

        self.scrollbar_horizontal = tk.Scrollbar(self.master, orient="horizontal", command=self.canvas.xview)
        self.scrollbar_horizontal.pack(side="bottom", fill="x")
        #self.canvas.configure(yscrollcommand=self.scrollbar_vertical.set, xscrollcommand=self.scrollbar_horizontal.set)
```

CONTROLLING VIDEO PLAYBACK

These methods (open_video(), play_video(), toggle_play_pause(), and stop_video()) are part of the Filter_CroppedFrame class. They handle various aspects of video playback and control in the graphical user interface (GUI) application implemented using Tkinter. Let's explain each method and its purpose:

open_video(self):
- This method is triggered when the user clicks on the "Open Video" button in the GUI.
- It opens a file dialog (filedialog.askopenfilename) to allow the user to select a video file (filetypes=[("Video files", "*.mp4;*.avi;*.mkv;*.wmv")]).

- If a video file (self.video_path) is selected:
    - imageio.get_reader(self.video_path) initializes self.video as an imageio reader object for the selected video file.
    - self.file_name extracts the filename from the full path (self.video_path.split('/')[-1]).
    - self.set_window_title() updates the GUI window title to reflect the selected video file.
    - self.number_of_frames = self.video.count_frames() retrieves and stores the total number of frames in the video.
    - self.play_video() automatically starts playing the video (self.paused set to False) and displays the first frame (self.show_frame()).

play_video(self):
- This method resumes playing the video if it's currently paused.
- Checks if self.video (the video reader object) exists:
- Sets self.paused to False, indicating that the video playback is not paused.
- Calls self.show_frame() to display the current frame of the video.

toggle_play_pause(self):
- Toggles between playing and pausing the video when the "Play/Pause" button is clicked.
- Checks if self.video exists:
    - Inverts the value of self.paused (self.paused = not self.paused), changing from playing to paused or vice versa.
    - If self.paused is False (indicating video should play), it calls self.play_video() to start playing the video.

stop_video(self):
- Stops the video playback and resets playback parameters when the "Stop" button is clicked.
- Sets self.paused to True, indicating that video playback is paused.
- Resets self.frame_index to 0, indicating the video should start from the beginning when played again.
- Clears self.bbox, likely a bounding box used for object detection or tracking.

- Calls self.show_frame() to display the first frame of the video, indicating it has stopped.

These methods collectively provide essential functionality for handling video playback within the GUI application. They allow users to open video files, play, pause, resume, and stop video playback seamlessly. This functionality enhances user interaction and facilitates real-time video analysis and processing tasks using the application's interface built with Tkinter.

```
def open_video(self):
    self.video_path = filedialog.askopenfilename(filetypes=[("Video files",
"*.mp4;*.avi;*.mkv;*.wmv")])
    if self.video_path:
        self.video = imageio.get_reader(self.video_path)
        self.file_name = self.video_path.split('/')[-1]
        self.set_window_title()
        self.number_of_frames = self.video.count_frames()
        self.play_video()  # Auto-play the video when opened
        self.show_frame()  # Show the first frame when the video is opened

def play_video(self):
    if self.video:
        self.paused = False
        self.show_frame()

def toggle_play_pause(self):
    if self.video:
        self.paused = not self.paused
        if not self.paused:
            self.play_video()  # If not paused, start playing

def stop_video(self):
    self.paused = True
    self.frame_index = 0
    self.bbox = None
    self.show_frame()
```

DISPLAYING AND UPDATING FRAME

The update_zoom() and show_frame() methods are integral parts of the Filter_CroppedFrame class. They handle updating the displayed frame in response to changes in zoom level and managing the video playback and display on the Tkinter canvas. Let's delve into each method and its functionality:

update_zoom(self, event=None):
- This method is called when there is a change in the zoom level selection, triggered by the user interacting with the zoom combobox.
- It simply calls self.show_frame() to update the displayed frame according to the new zoom level selected.

show_frame(self, auto_play=True):
- This method is responsible for displaying the current frame of the video on the Tkinter canvas.
- Checks if self.video (video reader object) exists:
  - If the video is not paused (not self.paused) or auto_play is False, it proceeds to display the frame.
  - Ensures that self.frame_index (current frame index) is within valid bounds (0 <= self.frame_index < self.number_of_frames).
  - Retrieves the current frame using self.video.get_data(self.frame_index) and converts it from RGB to BGR format using cv2.cvtColor(frame, cv2.COLOR_RGB2BGR).
  - Retrieves the current zoom scale (self.zoom_scale.get()) and resizes the frame accordingly (cv2.resize(frame, (int(width * zoom_value), int(height * zoom_value)))).
  - Converts the frame back to RGB format (cv2.cvtColor(frame, cv2.COLOR_BGR2RGB)) and creates a Tkinter-compatible PhotoImage (ImageTk.PhotoImage(frame)).
  - Stores the PhotoImage in self.photo and updates the canvas display: deletes any existing "video" tag (self.canvas.delete("video")) and creates a new image (self.canvas.create_image(0, 0, anchor="nw", image=photo, tags="video")) at the top-left corner (anchor="nw").
  - Updates the self.frame_number_label with the current frame index and total number of frames.
  - Adjusts the scroll region of the canvas to accommodate the new image size (self.canvas.config(scrollregion=self.canvas.bbox("all"))).
  - If auto_play is True, increments self.frame_index to display the next frame after a delay (self.master.after(30, self.show_frame)), effectively enabling continuous video playback at approximately 30 frames per second.

These methods collectively facilitate smooth and responsive video playback within the Tkinter GUI application. They handle dynamic updates in zoom level and ensure that the displayed frames are adjusted accordingly. This functionality enhances user interaction by providing real-time video visualization and analysis capabilities, supporting various video processing tasks that may involve object detection, tracking, or other forms of image manipulation.

```
def update_zoom(self, event=None):
    self.show_frame()

def show_frame(self, auto_play=True):
    if self.video:
        if not self.paused or not auto_play:
            if 0 <= self.frame_index < self.number_of_frames:
                frame = self.video.get_data(self.frame_index)
                frame = cv2.cvtColor(frame, cv2.COLOR_RGB2BGR)

                # Get the zoom scale value
                zoom_value = self.zoom_scale.get()

                height, width = frame.shape[:2]
                frame = cv2.resize(frame, (int(width * zoom_value), int(height * zoom_value)))

                frame = cv2.cvtColor(frame, cv2.COLOR_BGR2RGB)
                frame = Image.fromarray(frame)
                photo = ImageTk.PhotoImage(frame)
                self.photo = photo
                self.canvas.delete("video")
                self.canvas.create_image(0, 0, anchor="nw", image=photo, tags="video")

                self.frame_number_label.config(text=f"Frame: {self.frame_index} / {self.number_of_frames}", font=("Helvetica", 18))

                # Adjust the scroll region to the new image size
                self.canvas.config(scrollregion=self.canvas.bbox("all"))

                if auto_play:
                    self.frame_index += 1
                    self.master.after(30, self.show_frame)
```

NAVIGATING FRAMES

The prev_frame() and next_frame() methods are part of the Filter_CroppedFrame class. These methods handle navigation through frames of a video displayed in the Tkinter GUI. Let's explain each method and its purpose:

prev_frame(self):
- This method is called when the user clicks on the "Previous Frame" button in the GUI.
- Checks if the current self.frame_index is greater than 0 (if self.frame_index > 0), ensuring it does not go below the first frame.
- Decrements self.frame_index by 1 (self.frame_index -= 1).
- Calls self.show_frame(auto_play=False) to update the displayed frame without auto-playing the next frame, effectively showing the previous frame in the video sequence.

next_frame(self):
- This method is called when the user clicks on the "Next Frame" button in the GUI.
- Checks if self.video exists and ensures self.frame_index is less than self.number_of_frames - 1 (if self.video and self.frame_index < self.number_of_frames - 1), preventing it from advancing beyond the last frame of the video.
- Increments self.frame_index by 1 (self.frame_index += 1).
- Calls self.show_frame(auto_play=False) to update the displayed frame without auto-playing the next frame, effectively showing the next frame in the video sequence.

Purpose:
- Navigation Control: Both methods provide essential controls for navigating through the frames of the loaded video.
- Boundaries Checking: They ensure that the frame index (self.frame_index) stays within valid bounds (0 to self.number_of_frames - 1) to prevent accessing frames that do not exist.
- Frame Display Update: After adjusting self.frame_index, they call self.show_frame(auto_play=False) to update the GUI and display the corresponding frame on the canvas without automatically advancing to the next frame, which is useful for precise frame-by-frame analysis or user-directed navigation.

Usage:
- These methods are typically bound to corresponding buttons (self.prev_frame_button and self.next_frame_button) in the GUI created by the Filter_CroppedFrame class.
- They enhance user interaction by allowing intuitive navigation through video frames, supporting tasks such as manual inspection, frame selection, or verification in applications involving video processing, object tracking, or computer vision tasks.

```
def prev_frame(self):
    if self.frame_index > 0:
        self.frame_index -= 1
        self.show_frame(auto_play=False)

def next_frame(self):
    if self.video and self.frame_index < self.number_of_frames - 1:
        self.frame_index += 1
        self.show_frame(auto_play=False)
```

HANDLING MOUSE EVENTS

These methods (on_mousewheel(), on_press(), on_drag(), and on_release()) are additional functionalities within the Filter_CroppedFrame class, designed to enhance user interaction and provide additional features related to video frame manipulation and analysis. Let's go through each method to understand their purpose and functionality:

on_mousewheel(self, event):
- This method is triggered when the user scrolls the mouse wheel over the canvas displaying the video.
- event.delta gives the scroll direction and magnitude. Each "click" of the mouse wheel typically results in a change of event.delta by 120 units.
- Calculates direction based on event.delta // 120. Positive direction indicates scrolling up, and negative indicates scrolling down.
- Retrieves the current zoom scale value using self.zoom_scale.get().
- Adjusts current_value (zoom scale) based on the scroll direction:
  - If scrolling up (direction == 1) and current_value is less than 10, increments current_value by 1.
  - If scrolling down (direction == -1) and current_value is greater than 1, decrements current_value by 1.

- Sets the updated current_value back to self.zoom_scale using self.zoom_scale.set(current_value).
- Calls self.update_zoom() to update the displayed frame according to the new zoom scale.

on_press(self, event):
- Triggered when the user presses the mouse button (Button-1) on the canvas.
- event.x and event.y provide the coordinates of the mouse click relative to the canvas.
- Converts the canvas coordinates to screen coordinates (self.canvas.canvasx(event.x) and self.canvas.canvasy(event.y)) and stores them as self.start_x and self.start_y.
- Initializes self.bbox to None, indicating no bounding box selection is currently active.

on_drag(self, event):
- Activated when the user drags the mouse while holding down the mouse button (Button-1) on the canvas.
- event.x and event.y provide the current coordinates of the mouse drag event relative to the canvas.
- Calculates cur_x and cur_y as canvas coordinates (self.canvas.canvasx(event.x) and self.canvas.canvasy(event.y)).
- Deletes any existing self.bbox_rect (bounding box rectangle) on the canvas using self.canvas.delete(self.bbox_rect) if it exists.
- Updates self.bbox to define a bounding box from self.start_x, self.start_y (initial click position) to cur_x, cur_y (current drag position).
- Draws a new bounding box rectangle (self.bbox_rect) on the canvas with the updated coordinates, using a red outline (outline='#fc3d3d') and a width of 5 pixels.

on_release(self, event):
- Called when the user releases the mouse button (ButtonRelease-1) after a drag operation on the canvas.

- Invokes the analyze_histogram("NEW") method, passing the string "NEW" as an argument.
- This method call is intended to trigger an analysis process (likely related to histogram computation or some form of image processing) based on the newly defined bounding box (self.bbox) after the user releases the mouse button.

Purpose:
- Zoom Control (on_mousewheel): Enables users to zoom in and out of the video display using the mouse wheel, adjusting the displayed frame's size.
- Bounding Box Selection (on_press, on_drag, on_release): Facilitates interactive selection and visualization of bounding boxes on the video frames, useful for tasks like object detection, tracking, or region of interest (ROI) selection.
- User Interaction Enhancement: These methods enhance user interaction by providing intuitive controls for zooming and interactive selection, integrating these functionalities seamlessly within the Tkinter GUI application for video processing and analysis.

Integration:

These methods are typically bound to corresponding events (<MouseWheel>, <ButtonPress-1>, <B1-Motion>, <ButtonRelease-1>) on the Tkinter canvas (self.canvas), allowing users to interact directly with the video display area to perform zooming or define regions of interest for subsequent analysis or processing tasks.

```
def on_mousewheel(self, event):
    direction = event.delta // 120
    current_value = int(self.zoom_scale.get())
    if direction == 1 and current_value < 10:
        current_value += 1
    elif direction == -1 and current_value > 1:
        current_value -= 1
    self.zoom_scale.set(current_value)
    self.update_zoom()

def on_press(self, event):
    self.start_x = self.canvas.canvasx(event.x)
    self.start_y = self.canvas.canvasy(event.y)
    self.bbox = None

def on_drag(self, event):
    cur_x = self.canvas.canvasx(event.x)
    cur_y = self.canvas.canvasy(event.y)
    if self.bbox_rect:
```

```
            self.canvas.delete(self.bbox_rect)
        self.bbox = (self.start_x, self.start_y, cur_x, cur_y)
        self.bbox_rect = self.canvas.create_rectangle(*self.bbox, outline='#fc3d3d',
width=5)

    def on_release(self, event):
        self.analyze_histogram("NEW")  # Call analyze_histogram() method when the mouse
button is released
```

VISUALIZING HISTOGRAMS

These methods (analyze_histogram, display_cropped_image, display_histograms, display_line_histogram, display_bar_histogram, display_histogram_image, and plot_to_image) are integral to the functionality of the Filter_CroppedFrame class. They are responsible for analyzing video frames, displaying visualizations (such as histograms), and managing graphical elements within the Tkinter-based application. Let's explore each method and its role:

analyze_histogram(self, state):
- Checks if a bounding box (self.bbox) is defined.
- Converts canvas coordinates of the bounding box to frame coordinates.
- Retrieves the current zoom scale (self.zoom_scale.get()) and adjusts the bounding box dimensions accordingly.
- Retrieves the current frame from self.video.
- Crops the frame based on the adjusted bounding box coordinates.
- Calls update_filter_params(state) to obtain filter parameters based on the current state.
- Applies the selected filter (selected_filter) to the cropped frame using apply_filter.
- Calls create_popup_window to display a popup window with the filtered frame.
- Calls display_cropped_image and display_histograms to display the cropped image and its histograms respectively.

display_cropped_image(self, cropped_frame):
- Checks if cropped_frame is valid.
- Creates a Tkinter frame (cropped_frame_frame) within self.popup_window.
- Converts cropped_frame from BGR to RGB format (cv2.cvtColor).
- Resizes the image (self.cropped_img) to 600x600 pixels.
- Converts self.cropped_img to ImageTk.PhotoImage (cropped_photo).

- Creates a Tkinter canvas (cropped_canvas) to display cropped_photo.

display_histograms(self, cropped_frame):
- Creates a Tkinter frame (histograms_frame) within self.popup_window.
- Calls display_line_histogram and display_bar_histogram to display line and bar histograms respectively.

display_line_histogram(self, cropped_frame, histograms_frame):
- Clears all widgets within histograms_frame.
- Creates a new frame (line_histogram_frame) within histograms_frame.
- Initializes a matplotlib figure (fig) for line histogram visualization.
- Plots separate histograms for each RGB channel ('r', 'g', 'b') using cv2.calcHist.
- Converts the matplotlib plot to an image (line_histogram_img) using plot_to_image and displays it in line_histogram_frame.

display_bar_histogram(self, cropped_frame, histograms_frame):
- Creates a frame (bar_histogram_frame) within histograms_frame.
- Initializes a matplotlib figure (fig) for bar histogram visualization.
- Plots histograms for each RGB channel using np.histogram.
- Adds text annotations to the bars indicating histogram values.
- Converts the matplotlib plot to an image (bar_histogram_img) using plot_to_image and displays it in bar_histogram_frame.

display_histogram_image(self, parent_frame, img):
- Converts img (a matplotlib plot converted to ImageTk.PhotoImage) into a Tkinter canvas (histogram_canvas) within parent_frame.

plot_to_image(self, plt):
- Saves the current matplotlib plot (plt) as a temporary image file (temp_plot.png).
- Opens and returns this image as a PIL Image object (img).

Purpose:
- Histogram Analysis: analyze_histogram extracts and analyzes a specific region (self.bbox) of a video frame, applying selected filters and displaying results.
- Visualization: display_cropped_image and associated methods (display_histograms, display_line_histogram, display_bar_histogram) prepare and display visual representations of the cropped video frame and its histograms using Tkinter and matplotlib.
- Integration: These methods integrate video analysis, image processing, and GUI display within a Tkinter-based application, facilitating interactive exploration and analysis of video content and image data.

Usage:
- Interactive GUI: Users interact with the application to select regions of interest (self.bbox), apply filters, and visualize results through histograms and processed image displays.
- Real-time Updates: Changes in zoom scale or bounding box selection dynamically update visualizations, providing immediate feedback to the user.

These functionalities collectively enhance the utility and user experience of the video processing application implemented in the Filter_CroppedFrame class.

```
def analyze_histogram(self, state):
    if self.bbox is None:
        return

    x1, y1, x2, y2 = [int(self.canvas.canvasx(coord)) for coord in self.bbox]
    if x1 < x2 and y1 < y2:
        pass
    elif x1 > x2 and y1 > y2:
        x1, x2 = x2, x1
        y1, y2 = y2, y1
    elif x1 > x2 and y1 < y2:
        x1, x2 = x2, x1
    elif x1 < x2 and y1 > y2:
        y1, y2 = y2, y1

    zoom_value = self.zoom_scale.get()
    x1 //= zoom_value
    y1 //= zoom_value
    x2 //= zoom_value
    y2 //= zoom_value

    frame = self.video.get_data(self.frame_index)
```

```
        frame = cv2.cvtColor(frame, cv2.COLOR_RGB2BGR)

        if x1 < x2 and y1 < y2:
            cropped_frame = frame[y1:y2, x1:x2]
        else:
            return

        selected_filter = self.update_filter_params(state)

        # Apply selected filter
        self.filtered_frame  =  self.apply_filter(selected_filter,  cropped_frame,
self.filter_params)

        self.create_popup_window(self.filtered_frame, selected_filter)
        self.display_cropped_image(self.filtered_frame)
        self.display_histograms(self.filtered_frame)

    def display_cropped_image(self, cropped_frame):
        if cropped_frame is None:
            print("Error: Cropped frame is None.")
            return

        if cropped_frame.size == 0:
            print("Error: Cropped frame is empty.")
            return

        cropped_frame_frame = tk.Frame(self.popup_window)
        cropped_frame_frame.pack(side="left")

        # Ensure that the super-resolved image is in RGB format
        cropped_frame_rgb = cv2.cvtColor(cropped_frame, cv2.COLOR_BGR2RGB)

        cropped_img = Image.fromarray(cropped_frame_rgb)
        self.cropped_img = cropped_img.resize((600, 600))

        cropped_photo = ImageTk.PhotoImage(self.cropped_img)
        cropped_canvas = tk.Canvas(cropped_frame_frame, width=600, height=600)
        cropped_canvas.pack(side="left", anchor="nw")
        cropped_canvas.create_image(0, 0, anchor="nw", image=cropped_photo)
        cropped_canvas.image = cropped_photo

    def display_histograms(self, cropped_frame):
        histograms_frame = tk.Frame(self.popup_window)
        histograms_frame.pack(side="right", padx=20)

        self.display_line_histogram(cropped_frame, histograms_frame)
        self.display_bar_histogram(cropped_frame, histograms_frame)

    def display_line_histogram(self, cropped_frame, histograms_frame):
        # clears widget
        for widget in histograms_frame.winfo_children():
            widget.destroy()

        line_histogram_frame = tk.Frame(histograms_frame)
        line_histogram_frame.pack(side="top", pady=5)

        # Set the background color to a control-like color (light gray)
        control_bg_color = '#f0f0f0'
```

```python
        fig, ax = plt.subplots(figsize=(12, 4), facecolor=control_bg_color)
        ax.set_facecolor(control_bg_color)

        color = ('r', 'g', 'b')
        for i, col in enumerate(color):
            histr = cv2.calcHist([cropped_frame], [i], None, [256], [0, 256])
            plt.plot(histr, color=col, label=f'Channel {col.upper()}', linewidth=2)
            plt.xlim([0, 256])
        plt.title('Line Histogram')
        plt.xlabel('Pixel Value')
        plt.ylabel('Frequency')
        plt.tight_layout()
        plt.grid(True)
        plt.legend()

        line_histogram_img = self.plot_to_image(plt)
        self.display_histogram_image(line_histogram_frame, line_histogram_img)

    def display_bar_histogram(self, cropped_frame, histograms_frame):
        bar_histogram_frame = tk.Frame(histograms_frame)
        bar_histogram_frame.pack(side="bottom", pady=5)

        # Set the background color to a control-like color (light gray)
        control_bg_color = '#f0f0f0'

        # Create the figure and axes with the specified background color
        fig, ax = plt.subplots(figsize=(12, 4), facecolor=control_bg_color)
        ax.set_facecolor(control_bg_color)

        color = ('r', 'g', 'b')
        num_bars = 64
        for i, col in enumerate(color):
            hist_range = (0, 256)
            hist_counts, _ = np.histogram(cropped_frame[:, :, i], bins=num_bars, range=hist_range)
            ax.bar(np.arange(num_bars), hist_counts, color=col, alpha=0.7, label=f'Channel {col.upper()}')
            for index, value in enumerate(hist_counts):
                ax.text(index, value + 10, str(int(value)), ha='center', va='bottom', fontsize=9)

        ax.set_title('Bar Histogram')
        ax.set_xlabel('Pixel Value')
        ax.set_ylabel('Frequency')
        ax.set_xticks(np.linspace(0, num_bars-1, num=5))
        ax.set_xticklabels(np.linspace(0, 255, num=5, dtype=int))  # Adjust x-axis ticks
        ax.grid(True)
        ax.legend()
        plt.tight_layout()

        bar_histogram_img = self.plot_to_image(fig)
        self.display_histogram_image(bar_histogram_frame, bar_histogram_img)

    def display_histogram_image(self, parent_frame, img):
        histogram_photo = ImageTk.PhotoImage(image=img)
        histogram_canvas = tk.Canvas(parent_frame, width=900, height=300)
```

```
            histogram_canvas.pack(side="bottom", anchor="se")
            histogram_canvas.create_image(0, 0, anchor="nw", image=histogram_photo)
            histogram_canvas.image = histogram_photo

    def plot_histogram_bar_to_image(self, image):
        # Calculate histogram for each channel
        histograms = []
        for i in range(3):
            hist_range = (0, 256)
            hist_counts, _ = np.histogram(image[:, :, i], bins=64, range=hist_range)  # Adjust bins to 64
            histograms.append(hist_counts)

        # Extracting only 64 bins from the histogram
        num_bins = 64  # Adjusted to 64 bins

        # Generating colors for each channel
        colors = ['red', 'green', 'blue']

        plt.figure()
        for i, histogram in enumerate(histograms):
            # Normalize the histogram counts for better visualization
            hist_counts = histogram / np.sum(histogram)
            # Setting the color for each channel
            plt.bar(np.arange(num_bins),   hist_counts[:num_bins],   color=colors[i], alpha=0.7, label=f'Channel {["Red", "Green", "Blue"][i]}')

        plt.xlabel('Pixel Value')
        plt.ylabel('Normalized Frequency')
        plt.title('RGB Channel Histograms')
        plt.grid(True)
        plt.tight_layout()
        plt.legend()

        # Convert the histogram bar graph to an image
        histogram_bar_img = self.plot_to_image(plt)
        histogram_bar_photo = ImageTk.PhotoImage(image=histogram_bar_img)

        return histogram_bar_photo

    def plot_to_image(self, plt):
        plt.savefig('temp_plot.png')
        img = Image.open('temp_plot.png')
        return img
```

UPDATING FILTER PARAMETERS

The update_filter_params() method serves a crucial role in managing and adjusting parameters for various image processing filters within a graphical user interface (GUI). Its primary function is to synchronize user input with internal parameters (self.filter_params), ensuring that selected filters are applied with the correct settings to video frames or images. This method operates in response to user interactions with a combobox that allows them to select different image filters.

Upon invocation, the method first retrieves the currently selected filter type from the GUI's combobox (filter_combobox). This selection dictates which set of parameters need to be updated and applied when processing frames or images. The method initializes an empty dictionary (self.filter_params) that will store the parameters specific to the selected filter.

Depending on the selected filter type, such as "Gaussian", "Median", "Mean", "Bilateral Filtering", "Non-local Means Denoising", "Anisotropic Diffusion", "Total Variation Denoising", "Haar Wavelet Transform", "Adaptive Thresholding", or "Wiener Filter", the method fetches corresponding parameters from the GUI widgets (parameter_widgets). These parameters include values such as kernel sizes, sigma values, thresholds, and others essential for each filter's operation.

Once the method has retrieved the necessary parameters based on the selected filter type, it updates self.filter_params accordingly. This ensures that when the filter is applied to a cropped frame or an image, it uses the most current and accurate parameter values set by the user through the GUI. After updating self.filter_params, the method also updates the GUI widgets to reflect these changes, providing real-time feedback to the user about the current parameter settings.

The GUI widgets are updated by clearing their current contents and inserting the updated parameter values. This synchronization process ensures that the GUI accurately represents the parameters being applied to the filters, maintaining consistency between user input and internal processing logic.

Upon completion of parameter updates and GUI synchronization, the method returns the selected filter type (selected_filter). This return value signifies the active filter type and its associated parameters, allowing other parts of the application to apply the selected filter with the correct settings.

Overall, the update_filter_params() method enhances user interaction by facilitating intuitive adjustment of filter parameters through a GUI interface. It optimizes the application of image processing techniques by ensuring that filters are applied with precise and up-to-date configurations, thereby enhancing the quality and flexibility of image and video processing workflows.

This method's implementation underscores its role in bridging user input with backend processing, thereby enriching the interactive experience and functionality of the application. It encapsulates the workflow of parameter management for diverse image filters, promoting ease of use and effectiveness in applying advanced image processing techniques.

```
    def update_filter_params(self, state):
        # Get selected filter from combobox
        selected_filter = self.filter_combobox.get()
        self.filter_params = {}
        if state != "NEW" and selected_filter=="Gaussian":
            self.kernel_gaussian_val                                     = int(self.parameter_widgets["kernel_size_gaussian"].get())
            self.sigma_gaussian_val                                      = float(self.parameter_widgets["sigma_gaussian"].get())

            # Define filter parameters as a dictionary
            self.filter_params = {"kernel_size_gaussian": self.kernel_gaussian_val, "sigma_gaussian": self.sigma_gaussian_val}

            # Updates Gaussian Filter Params
            self.kernel_gaussian.delete(0, tk.END)
            self.sigma_gaussian.delete(0, tk.END)
            self.kernel_gaussian.insert(0, str(self.kernel_gaussian_val))
            self.sigma_gaussian.insert(0, str(self.sigma_gaussian_val))

        if state != "NEW" and selected_filter=="Median":
            self.kernel_median_val                                       = int(self.parameter_widgets["kernel_size_median"].get())
            # Define filter parameters as a dictionary
            self.filter_params = {"kernel_size_median": self.kernel_median_val}

            #Median Filter Param
            self.kernel_median.delete(0, tk.END)
            self.kernel_median.insert(0, str(self.kernel_median_val))

        if state != "NEW" and selected_filter=="Mean":
            self.kernel_mean_val                                         = int(self.parameter_widgets["kernel_size_mean"].get())
            # Define filter parameters as a dictionary
            self.filter_params = {"kernel_size_mean": self.kernel_mean_val}

            #Mean Filter Param
            self.kernel_mean.delete(0, tk.END)
            self.kernel_mean.insert(0, str(self.kernel_mean_val))

        if state != "NEW" and selected_filter == "Bilateral Filtering":
            # Get the parameter values from the corresponding widgets
            d = int(self.parameter_widgets["d_bilateral"].get())
            sigma_color = float(self.parameter_widgets["sigma_color_bilateral"].get())
            sigma_space = float(self.parameter_widgets["sigma_space_bilateral"].get())

            # Define filter parameters as a dictionary
            self.filter_params    =    {"d_bilateral":    d,    "sigma_color_bilateral": sigma_color, "sigma_space_bilateral": sigma_space}

            # Updates Bilateral Filter Params
```

```
            self.d_bilateral.delete(0, tk.END)
            self.sigma_color_bilateral.delete(0, tk.END)
            self.sigma_space_bilateral.delete(0, tk.END)
            self.d_bilateral.insert(0, str(d))
            self.sigma_color_bilateral.insert(0, str(sigma_color))
            self.sigma_space_bilateral.insert(0, str(sigma_space))

        if state != "NEW" and selected_filter == "Non-local Means Denoising":
            self.h_val = float(self.parameter_widgets["h_denoising"].get())
            self.hForColor_val                                                    =
float(self.parameter_widgets["hForColor_denoising"].get())
            self.templateWindowSize_val                                           =
int(self.parameter_widgets["templateWindowSize_denoising"].get())
            self.searchWindowSize_val                                             =
int(self.parameter_widgets["searchWindowSize_denoising"].get())

            # Define filter parameters as a dictionary
            self.filter_params = {
                "h": self.h_val,
                "hForColor": self.hForColor_val,
                "templateWindowSize": self.templateWindowSize_val,
                "searchWindowSize": self.searchWindowSize_val
            }

            # Update filter params in the GUI
            self.parameter_widgets["h_denoising"].delete(0, tk.END)
            self.parameter_widgets["hForColor_denoising"].delete(0, tk.END)
            self.parameter_widgets["templateWindowSize_denoising"].delete(0, tk.END)
            self.parameter_widgets["searchWindowSize_denoising"].delete(0, tk.END)

            self.parameter_widgets["h_denoising"].insert(0, str(self.h_val))
            self.parameter_widgets["hForColor_denoising"].insert(0,
str(self.hForColor_val))
            self.parameter_widgets["templateWindowSize_denoising"].insert(0,
str(self.templateWindowSize_val))
            self.parameter_widgets["searchWindowSize_denoising"].insert(0,
str(self.searchWindowSize_val))

        if state != "NEW" and selected_filter == "Anisotropic Diffusion":
            self.num_iterations_val                                               =
int(self.parameter_widgets["num_iterations_diffusion"].get())
            self.kappa_val = float(self.parameter_widgets["kappa_diffusion"].get())
            self.gamma_val = float(self.parameter_widgets["gamma_diffusion"].get())
            self.option_val = int(self.parameter_widgets["option_diffusion"].get())

            # Define filter parameters as a dictionary
            self.filter_params = {
                "num_iterations": self.num_iterations_val,
                "kappa": self.kappa_val,
                "gamma": self.gamma_val,
                "option": self.option_val
            }

            # Update filter params in the GUI
            self.parameter_widgets["num_iterations_diffusion"].delete(0, tk.END)
            self.parameter_widgets["kappa_diffusion"].delete(0, tk.END)
            self.parameter_widgets["gamma_diffusion"].delete(0, tk.END)
            self.parameter_widgets["option_diffusion"].delete(0, tk.END)
```

```python
            self.parameter_widgets["num_iterations_diffusion"].insert(0, str(self.num_iterations_val))
            self.parameter_widgets["kappa_diffusion"].insert(0, str(self.kappa_val))
            self.parameter_widgets["gamma_diffusion"].insert(0, str(self.gamma_val))
            self.parameter_widgets["option_diffusion"].insert(0, str(self.option_val))

        if state != "NEW" and selected_filter == "Total Variation Denoising":
            self.weight_val = float(self.parameter_widgets["weight_denoising"].get())
            self.iterations_val = int(self.parameter_widgets["iterations_denoising"].get())

            # Define filter parameters as a dictionary
            self.filter_params = {
                "weight": self.weight_val,
                "iterations": self.iterations_val
            }

            # Update filter params in the GUI
            self.parameter_widgets["weight_denoising"].delete(0, tk.END)
            self.parameter_widgets["iterations_denoising"].delete(0, tk.END)

            self.parameter_widgets["weight_denoising"].insert(0, str(self.weight_val))
            self.parameter_widgets["iterations_denoising"].insert(0, str(self.iterations_val))

        if state != "NEW" and selected_filter == "Haar Wavelet Transform":
            self.wavelet_val = self.parameter_widgets["wavelet_type"].get()
            self.level_val = int(self.parameter_widgets["wavelet_level"].get())

            # Define filter parameters as a dictionary
            self.filter_params = {
                "wavelet": self.wavelet_val,
                "level": self.level_val
            }

            # Update filter params in the GUI
            self.parameter_widgets["wavelet_type"].delete(0, tk.END)
            self.parameter_widgets["wavelet_level"].delete(0, tk.END)

            self.parameter_widgets["wavelet_type"].insert(0, str(self.wavelet_val))
            self.parameter_widgets["wavelet_level"].insert(0, str(self.level_val))

        if state != "NEW" and selected_filter == "Haar Wavelet Transform":
            self.wavelet_val = self.parameter_widgets["wavelet_type"].get()
            self.level_val = int(self.parameter_widgets["wavelet_level"].get())
            self.threshold_val = float(self.parameter_widgets["threshold"].get())

            # Define filter parameters as a dictionary
            self.filter_params = {
                "wavelet": self.wavelet_val,
                "level": self.level_val,
                "threshold": self.threshold_val
            }

            # Update filter params in the GUI
```

```python
            self.parameter_widgets["wavelet_type"].delete(0, tk.END)
            self.parameter_widgets["wavelet_level"].delete(0, tk.END)
            self.parameter_widgets["threshold"].delete(0, tk.END)

            self.parameter_widgets["wavelet_type"].insert(0, str(self.wavelet_val))
            self.parameter_widgets["wavelet_level"].insert(0, str(self.level_val))
            self.parameter_widgets["threshold"].insert(0, str(self.threshold_val))

        if state != "NEW" and selected_filter == "Adaptive Thresholding":
            self.block_size_val = int(self.parameter_widgets["block_size"].get())
            self.c_val = int(self.parameter_widgets["c"].get())
            self.adaptive_method_val = self.parameter_widgets["adaptive_method"].get()
            self.threshold_type_val = self.parameter_widgets["threshold_type"].get()

            # Map adaptive method string value to integer value
            adaptive_methods            =            {"cv2.ADAPTIVE_THRESH_MEAN_C":
cv2.ADAPTIVE_THRESH_MEAN_C,
                        "cv2.ADAPTIVE_THRESH_GAUSSIAN_C":
cv2.ADAPTIVE_THRESH_GAUSSIAN_C}
            self.adaptive_method_val = adaptive_methods.get(self.adaptive_method_val)

            # Map threshold type string value to integer value
            threshold_types = {"cv2.THRESH_BINARY": cv2.THRESH_BINARY,
                        "cv2.THRESH_BINARY_INV": cv2.THRESH_BINARY_INV}
            self.threshold_type_val = threshold_types.get(self.threshold_type_val)

            # Define filter parameters as a dictionary
            self.filter_params = {
                "block_size": self.block_size_val,
                "C": self.c_val,
                "adaptive_method": self.adaptive_method_val,
                "threshold_type": self.threshold_type_val
            }

            # Update filter params in the GUI
            self.parameter_widgets["block_size"].delete(0, tk.END)
            self.parameter_widgets["c"].delete(0, tk.END)
            # Use set method with the correct syntax
self.parameter_widgets["adaptive_method"].set(str(self.adaptive_method_val))

self.parameter_widgets["threshold_type"].set(str(self.threshold_type_val))

            self.parameter_widgets["block_size"].insert(0, str(self.block_size_val))
            self.parameter_widgets["c"].insert(0, str(self.c_val))

        if state != "NEW" and selected_filter == "Wiener Filter":
            self.kernel_size_val = int(self.parameter_widgets["kernel_size"].get())
            self.noise_var_val = float(self.parameter_widgets["noise_var"].get())

            # Define filter parameters as a dictionary
            self.filter_params = {
                "kernel_size": self.kernel_size_val,
                "noise_var": self.noise_var_val
            }

            # Update filter params in the GUI
            self.parameter_widgets["kernel_size"].delete(0, tk.END)
```

```
        self.parameter_widgets["noise_var"].delete(0, tk.END)
        self.parameter_widgets["kernel_size"].insert(0,
str(self.kernel_size_val))
        self.parameter_widgets["noise_var"].insert(0, str(self.noise_var_val))

    return selected_filter
```

ACCESSING FILTERS PARAMETERS

1. Bilateral Filter Parameters: The get_bilateral_params function retrieves parameters needed for bilateral filtering, which is effective for noise reduction while preserving edges in an image. It checks if d_bilateral, sigma_color_bilateral, and sigma_space_bilateral are present in filter_params. If any of these parameters are missing, default values of 9 for d, and 75 for both color and space are assigned. These values control the pixel neighborhood diameter and the sigma values for color and spatial distances, respectively.
2. Gaussian Filter Parameters: For Gaussian filtering, used commonly for smoothing and noise reduction, the get_gaussian_params function retrieves kernel_size and sigma from filter_params. kernel_size determines the size of the Gaussian kernel, while sigma controls the spread of the Gaussian distribution. Default values of 5 for kernel_size and 0.1 for sigma are provided if not specified in filter_params.
3. Median Filter Parameters: The get_median_params function retrieves the kernel_size parameter from filter_params for median filtering, which helps in reducing noise by replacing each pixel value with the median of its neighborhood. If kernel_size is not defined, it defaults to 5.
4. Mean Filter Parameters: Similar to median filtering, the get_mean_params function retrieves kernel_size from filter_params for mean filtering. This filter replaces each pixel value with the average of its neighborhood pixels. If kernel_size is absent, it defaults to 5.
5. Non-local Means Denoising Parameters: The get_nlm_denoising_params function fetches parameters (h, hForColor, templateWindowSize, searchWindowSize) for non-local means denoising, which is effective in preserving image details while reducing noise. Default values of 10 for h and hForColor, 7 for templateWindowSize, and 21 for searchWindowSize are used if not provided in filter_params.
6. Anisotropic Diffusion Parameters: Anisotropic diffusion, implemented through the get_diffusion_params function, smooths images while preserving edges. It retrieves parameters (num_iterations, kappa, gamma, option) controlling diffusion

iterations, diffusion coefficient, gradient factor, and processing option. Default values are 10, 15, 0.2, and 1 respectively, if not specified.
7. Total Variation Denoising Parameters: For total variation denoising, which effectively removes noise while preserving edges, the get_total_variation_params function retrieves weight and iterations from filter_params. These parameters control the weight factor and the number of iterations for denoising. Default values are 0.01 for weight and 20 for iterations if not explicitly set.
8. Haar Wavelet Transform Parameters: The get_haar_wavelet_params function retrieves parameters (wavelet, level, threshold) used in Haar wavelet transforms, often applied in signal and image processing for compression and denoising. Default values are "haar" for wavelet, 1 for level, and 0.0 for threshold if not specified.
9. Adaptive Thresholding Parameters: For adaptive thresholding, essential in image segmentation, the get_adaptive_thresholding_params function fetches parameters (block_size, C, adaptive_method, threshold_type). These parameters define the block size, constant subtraction value, adaptive method, and threshold type (mean or Gaussian). Default values are 11 for block_size, 2 for C, cv2.ADAPTIVE_THRESH_MEAN_C for adaptive_method, and cv2.THRESH_BINARY for threshold_type if not specified.
10. Wiener Filter Parameters: Lastly, the get_wiener_filter_params function retrieves kernel_size and noise_var parameters for the Wiener filter, which is effective in reducing noise from images. kernel_size specifies the size of the filter kernel, and noise_var denotes the noise variance. Default values are 5 for kernel_size and 0.01 for noise_var if not provided.

These functions are designed to ensure that each image processing filter has access to its required parameters, providing flexibility through default values when specific parameters are not explicitly defined. This approach enables robust implementation of various filtering techniques tailored to different image enhancement and denoising tasks.

```
def get_bilateral_params(self, filter_params):
    if "d_bilateral" in filter_params:
        d = filter_params["d_bilateral"]
    else:
        # default value
        d = 9

    if "sigma_color_bilateral" in filter_params:
        color = filter_params["sigma_color_bilateral"]
    else:
        # default value
```

```python
            color = 75

        if "sigma_space_bilateral" in filter_params:
            space = filter_params["sigma_space_bilateral"]
        else:
            # default value
            space = 75

        return d, color, space

    def get_gaussian_params(self, filter_params):
        if "kernel_size_gaussian" in filter_params:
            kernel_size = filter_params["kernel_size_gaussian"]
        else:
            # default value
            kernel_size = 5

        if "sigma_gaussian" in filter_params:
            sigma = filter_params["sigma_gaussian"]
        else:
            # default value
            sigma = 0.1

        return kernel_size, sigma

    def get_median_params(self, filter_params):
        if "kernel_size_median" in filter_params:
            kernel_size = filter_params["kernel_size_median"]
        else:
            # default value
            kernel_size = 5
        return kernel_size

    def get_mean_params(self, filter_params):
        if "kernel_size_mean" in filter_params:
            kernel_size = filter_params["kernel_size_mean"]
        else:
            # default value
            kernel_size = 5
        return kernel_size

    def get_nlm_denoising_params(self, filter_params):
        h = filter_params.get("h", 10)  # default value 10
        hForColor = filter_params.get("hForColor", 10)  # default value 10
        templateWindowSize = filter_params.get("templateWindowSize", 7)   # default value 7
        searchWindowSize = filter_params.get("searchWindowSize", 21)  # default value 21

        return h, hForColor, templateWindowSize, searchWindowSize

    def get_diffusion_params(self, filter_params):
        num_iterations = filter_params.get("num_iterations", 10)  # default value 10
        kappa = filter_params.get("kappa", 15)  # default value 15
        gamma = filter_params.get("gamma", 0.2)  # default value 0.2
        option = filter_params.get("option", 1)  # default value 1
        return num_iterations, kappa, gamma, option

    def get_total_variation_params(self, filter_params):
```

```python
        weight = filter_params.get("weight", 0.01)  # default value 0.01
        iterations = filter_params.get("iterations", 20)  # default value 20
        return weight, iterations

    def get_haar_wavelet_params(self, filter_params):
        wavelet = filter_params.get("wavelet", "haar")  # default value "haar"
        level = filter_params.get("level", 1)  # default value 1
        threshold = filter_params.get("threshold", 0.0)  # default value 0.0
        return wavelet, level, threshold

    def get_adaptive_thresholding_params(self, filter_params):
        block_size = filter_params.get("block_size", 11)  # default value 11
        C = filter_params.get("C", 2)  # default value 2
        adaptive_method = filter_params.get("adaptive_method", cv2.ADAPTIVE_THRESH_MEAN_C)  # default value cv2.ADAPTIVE_THRESH_MEAN_C
        threshold_type = filter_params.get("threshold_type", cv2.THRESH_BINARY)  # default value cv2.THRESH_BINARY
        return block_size, C, adaptive_method, threshold_type

    def get_wiener_filter_params(self, filter_params):
        kernel_size = filter_params.get("kernel_size", 5)  # default value 5
        noise_var = filter_params.get("noise_var", 0.01)  # default value 0.01
        return kernel_size, noise_var
```

DEFINING FILTERS

These functions provide essential image processing capabilities, each tailored to specific tasks such as noise reduction, adaptive thresholding, and wavelet-based denoising. They incorporate checks for input validity, apply advanced algorithms effectively, and ensure output quality through parameter tuning and iterative processing.

1. Wiener Filter Function: The wiener_filter function is designed to reduce noise from an input image frame using the Wiener filtering technique. It first checks the validity of the input frame by ensuring it is not None, is a valid NumPy array, and is not empty. Additionally, it verifies that the frame is in BGR color space. If any of these conditions are not met, appropriate error messages are printed, and None is returned. If the frame passes these checks, the function proceeds by applying median blurring with a specified kernel_size to the frame to mitigate noise. Subsequently, it applies fast non-local means denoising with a specified noise_var parameter. The resulting filtered frame is then returned.

2. Adaptive Thresholding for Each Channel Function: The adaptive_threshold_each_channel function performs adaptive thresholding separately on each color channel (blue, green, red) of an input frame. It first splits the frame into these individual channels using OpenCV's cv2.split function. Then, adaptive thresholding is applied to each channel using parameters such as block_size, C (constant subtracted from the mean or weighted mean),

adaptive_method (adaptive thresholding method), and threshold_type (type of thresholding operation). The function returns a merged image where each channel has undergone adaptive thresholding independently, enhancing contrast and clarity in segmented areas of the image.

3. Haar Wavelet Transform Function: The haar_wavelet_transform function utilizes the Haar wavelet transform technique to decompose each color channel (blue, green, red) of an input image frame into wavelet coefficients. These coefficients are thresholded to remove noise and retain significant image features. The function begins by splitting the frame into its individual color channels and applies wavelet decomposition (pywt.wavedec2) using the specified wavelet type and decomposition level. After thresholding the detail coefficients with a given threshold, it reconstructs each channel using inverse wavelet transform (pywt.waverec2). Finally, the function ensures the pixel values are clipped within the valid range and merges the denoised channels to produce a cleaner image.

4. Daubechies Wavelet Transform Function: The daubechies_wavelet_transform function performs the Daubechies wavelet transform, specifically using the Daubechies 5 wavelet function (db5). It operates similarly to the Haar wavelet transform but with a different wavelet basis. The function begins by splitting the input image frame into its constituent color channels (blue, green, red). It then applies 2D wavelet transform (pywt.dwt2) to each channel, decomposing it into wavelet coefficients. These coefficients undergo inverse wavelet transform (pywt.idwt2) to reconstruct the channels, effectively reducing noise while preserving image details. The function ensures the resultant pixel values are within the valid range by clipping them and returns the denoised image as a merged RGB frame.

5. Anisotropic Diffusion Function: The anisotropic_diffusion function implements anisotropic diffusion, a technique used for edge-preserving image smoothing. This method iteratively updates each pixel in the input image (img) over a specified number of num_iterations. Parameters such as kappa (diffusion coefficient), gamma (time step), and option (diffusion option) govern the diffusion process. Depending on the chosen option, the function computes gradient-based diffusion coefficients and updates the image pixels accordingly. After completing the specified number of iterations, the function returns the processed image with reduced noise and preserved edges.

6. Total Variation Denoising Function: The total_variation_denoising function applies total variation denoising to an input RGB image (img). This denoising technique effectively removes noise while preserving edges and image structures.

The function first splits the input image into its individual color channels (blue, green, red). It then applies total variation denoising (apply_total_variation_denoising_channel) to each channel separately using parameters such as weight (denoising weight) and iterations (number of denoising iterations). The denoised channels are merged back together to produce a clean RGB image. By iteratively updating pixel values based on the gradient of the image, total variation denoising enhances image quality and sharpness.

```
def wiener_filter(self, frame, kernel_size=5, noise_var=0.01):
    # Check if frame is None
    if frame is None:
        print("Error: Input frame is None.")
        return None

    # Check if frame is a valid numpy array
    if not isinstance(frame, np.ndarray):
        print("Error: Input frame is not a numpy array.")
        return None

    # Check if frame is an empty array
    if frame.size == 0:
        print("Error: Input frame is empty.")
        return None

    # Check if frame is in BGR color space
    if frame.shape[-1] != 3:
        print("Error: Input frame is not in BGR color space.")
        return None

    # Apply Wiener filter
    filtered_frame = cv2.medianBlur(frame, kernel_size)  # Use kernel_size[0] as the kernel size
    filtered_frame = cv2.fastNlMeansDenoising(filtered_frame, h=noise_var)
    return filtered_frame

def adaptive_threshold_each_channel(self, frame, block_size, C, adaptive_method, threshold_type):
    # Split the frame into individual channels
    b, g, r = cv2.split(frame)

    # Apply adaptive thresholding to each channel separately
    b_thresh = cv2.adaptiveThreshold(b, 255, adaptive_method, threshold_type, block_size, C)
    g_thresh = cv2.adaptiveThreshold(g, 255, adaptive_method, threshold_type, block_size, C)
    r_thresh = cv2.adaptiveThreshold(r, 255, adaptive_method, threshold_type, block_size, C)

    # Merge the thresholded channels back together
    return cv2.merge([b_thresh, g_thresh, r_thresh])
```

```python
def haar_wavelet_transform(self, frame, wavelet='haar', level=1, threshold=0.1):
    def threshold_coeffs(coeffs, threshold):
        cA, (cH, cV, cD) = coeffs
        cH = pywt.threshold(cH, threshold, mode='soft')
        cV = pywt.threshold(cV, threshold, mode='soft')
        cD = pywt.threshold(cD, threshold, mode='soft')
        return cA, (cH, cV, cD)

    # Split the frame into its individual color channels
    b, g, r = cv2.split(frame)

    # Perform the wavelet transform and thresholding on each channel separately
    b_coeffs = pywt.wavedec2(b, wavelet, level=level)
    g_coeffs = pywt.wavedec2(g, wavelet, level=level)
    r_coeffs = pywt.wavedec2(r, wavelet, level=level)

    # Apply thresholding to the detail coefficients
    b_coeffs = threshold_coeffs(b_coeffs, threshold)
    g_coeffs = threshold_coeffs(g_coeffs, threshold)
    r_coeffs = threshold_coeffs(r_coeffs, threshold)

    # Reconstruct the channels from the coefficients
    b_reconstructed = pywt.waverec2(b_coeffs, wavelet)
    g_reconstructed = pywt.waverec2(g_coeffs, wavelet)
    r_reconstructed = pywt.waverec2(r_coeffs, wavelet)

    # Clip the values to ensure they are within the valid range
    b_reconstructed = np.clip(b_reconstructed, 0, 255).astype(np.uint8)
    g_reconstructed = np.clip(g_reconstructed, 0, 255).astype(np.uint8)
    r_reconstructed = np.clip(r_reconstructed, 0, 255).astype(np.uint8)

    # Merge the channels back together
    return cv2.merge([b_reconstructed, g_reconstructed, r_reconstructed])

def daubechies_wavelet_transform(self, frame):
    # Split the frame into its individual color channels
    b, g, r = cv2.split(frame)

    # Choose the wavelet function (Daubechies 5)
    wavelet = 'db5'

    # Perform the wavelet transform on each channel separately
    b_coeffs = pywt.dwt2(b, wavelet)
    g_coeffs = pywt.dwt2(g, wavelet)
    r_coeffs = pywt.dwt2(r, wavelet)

    # Reconstruct the channels from the coefficients
    b_reconstructed = pywt.idwt2(b_coeffs, wavelet)
    g_reconstructed = pywt.idwt2(g_coeffs, wavelet)
    r_reconstructed = pywt.idwt2(r_coeffs, wavelet)

    # Clip the values to ensure they are within the valid range
    b_reconstructed = np.clip(b_reconstructed, 0, 255).astype(np.uint8)
    g_reconstructed = np.clip(g_reconstructed, 0, 255).astype(np.uint8)
    r_reconstructed = np.clip(r_reconstructed, 0, 255).astype(np.uint8)

    # Merge the channels back together
    return cv2.merge([b_reconstructed, g_reconstructed, r_reconstructed])
```

```python
    def anisotropic_diffusion(self, img, num_iterations=10, kappa=15, gamma=0.2, option=1):
        img = img.astype(np.float32)
        for i in range(num_iterations):
            # Compute gradients
            gradient_north = np.roll(img, -1, axis=0) - img
            gradient_south = np.roll(img, 1, axis=0) - img
            gradient_east = np.roll(img, -1, axis=1) - img
            gradient_west = np.roll(img, 1, axis=1) - img

            # Compute the diffusion coefficients based on gradient magnitude
            if option == 1:
                c_north = np.exp(-(gradient_north / kappa) ** 2)
                c_south = np.exp(-(gradient_south / kappa) ** 2)
                c_east = np.exp(-(gradient_east / kappa) ** 2)
                c_west = np.exp(-(gradient_west / kappa) ** 2)
            elif option == 2:
                c_north = 1 / (1 + (gradient_north / kappa) ** 2)
                c_south = 1 / (1 + (gradient_south / kappa) ** 2)
                c_east = 1 / (1 + (gradient_east / kappa) ** 2)
                c_west = 1 / (1 + (gradient_west / kappa) ** 2)

            # Update image
            img += gamma * (c_north * gradient_north + c_south * gradient_south + c_east * gradient_east + c_west * gradient_west)

        return img.astype(np.uint8)

    def apply_total_variation_denoising_channel(self, channel, weight, iterations):
        # Initialize the result with the original channel
        result = channel.copy().astype(np.float64)  # Convert to float64

        # Perform total variation denoising
        for _ in range(iterations):
            # Compute the gradient of the channel
            dx = cv2.Sobel(result, cv2.CV_64F, 1, 0, ksize=3)
            dy = cv2.Sobel(result, cv2.CV_64F, 0, 1, ksize=3)

            # Update the channel using the gradient and the weight
            result -= weight * np.sqrt(dx**2 + dy**2)

        # Clip the values to ensure they are within the valid range
        result = np.clip(result, 0, 255).astype(np.uint8)

        return result

    def total_variation_denoising(self, img, weight=0.01, iterations=20):
        # Split the image into its individual color channels
        b, g, r = cv2.split(img)

        # Apply total variation denoising to each channel separately
        b_denoised = self.apply_total_variation_denoising_channel(b, weight, iterations)
        g_denoised = self.apply_total_variation_denoising_channel(g, weight, iterations)
        r_denoised = self.apply_total_variation_denoising_channel(r, weight, iterations)
```

```
# Merge the denoised channels back together
return cv2.merge([b_denoised, g_denoised, r_denoised])
```

CHOOSING FILTER

The apply_filter() method is a versatile function designed to apply various image processing filters to an input frame based on the specified filter_name and optional filter_params. It begins by checking if filter_params is None; if so, it initializes it as an empty dictionary to avoid potential errors with uninitialized parameters. The method then uses a series of conditional statements (if-elif) to determine which filter to apply based on the provided filter_name.

1. Initial Checks: If filter_name is "None", indicating no filter should be applied, the method simply returns the original input frame without any modifications.
2. Gaussian Blur: If filter_name is "Gaussian", it retrieves the kernel_size and sigma parameters using the get_gaussian_params method. These parameters control the size of the Gaussian kernel and the standard deviation in the x and y directions. It applies cv2.GaussianBlur to smooth the image, reducing noise while preserving edges.
3. Mean Blur: For "Mean" filtering, the method calls get_mean_params to fetch the kernel_size, which defines the size of the square kernel. It then applies cv2.blur (mean filtering), averaging pixel values within the kernel to achieve smoothing, useful for reducing uniform noise.
4. Median Blur: When filter_name is "Median", it retrieves the kernel_size using get_median_params. This size specifies the aperture size for median filtering (cv2.medianBlur), which replaces each pixel value with the median value under the kernel area. Median filtering is effective against salt-and-pepper noise.
5. Bilateral Filtering: For "Bilateral Filtering", the method obtains d, color, and space parameters via get_bilateral_params. These parameters control the spatial and color domains for cv2.bilateralFilter, preserving edges while reducing noise. It's particularly useful for smoothing images without losing important details.
6. Non-local Means Denoising: When filter_name is "Non-local Means Denoising", it retrieves parameters such as h, hForColor, templateWindowSize, and searchWindowSize using get_nlm_denoising_params. These parameters influence cv2.fastNlMeansDenoisingColored, which applies non-local means denoising to colored images, effectively reducing noise while preserving image details.
7. Anisotropic Diffusion: If filter_name is "Anisotropic Diffusion", it fetches parameters like num_iterations, kappa, gamma, and option using

get_diffusion_params. These parameters are used in the anisotropic_diffusion function to perform edge-preserving smoothing, beneficial for retaining sharp edges while removing noise over multiple iterations.
8. Total Variation Denoising: When filter_name is "Total Variation Denoising", it retrieves weight and iterations using get_total_variation_params. These parameters govern the amount of regularization applied in total_variation_denoising, effectively removing noise while preserving image structure and sharpness.
9. Wiener Filter: For "Wiener Filter", the method retrieves kernel_size and noise_var parameters using get_wiener_filter_params. These parameters influence wiener_filter, which employs Wiener filtering to reduce noise in the image, particularly effective when the noise characteristics are known.
10. Adaptive Thresholding and Wavelet Transforms: Lastly, if filter_name corresponds to "Adaptive Thresholding", "Haar Wavelet Transform", or "Daubechies Wavelet Transform", the method fetches respective parameters using dedicated get_*_params methods. It then applies the corresponding image processing techniques (adaptive_threshold_each_channel, haar_wavelet_transform, daubechies_wavelet_transform) to enhance image quality or transform the image into a different domain based on the selected wavelet function.

Each conditional branch ensures that the appropriate filter or transformation is applied to the input frame based on the specified filter_name. If the filter_name does not match any predefined options, the method defaults to returning the original input frame, ensuring robustness and reliability in handling unexpected filter names. This approach allows for flexible and efficient image processing tailored to different noise reduction and transformation needs.

```
def apply_filter(self, filter_name, frame, filter_params=None):
    if filter_params is None:
        filter_params = {}
    if filter_name == "None":
        return frame
    elif filter_name == "Gaussian":
        kernel_size, sigma = self.get_gaussian_params(filter_params)
        return cv2.GaussianBlur(frame, (kernel_size,kernel_size), sigma)
    elif filter_name == "Mean":
        kernel_size = self.get_mean_params(filter_params)
        return cv2.blur(frame, (kernel_size, kernel_size))
    elif filter_name == "Median":
        kernel_size = self.get_median_params(filter_params)
        return cv2.medianBlur(frame, kernel_size)
```

```
        elif filter_name == "Bilateral Filtering":
            d, color, space = self.get_bilateral_params(filter_params)
            return cv2.bilateralFilter(frame, d, color, space)
        elif filter_name == "Non-local Means Denoising":
            h,       hForColor,     templateWindowSize,    searchWindowSize    =
self.get_nlm_denoising_params(filter_params)
            return   cv2.fastNlMeansDenoisingColored(frame,   None,   h,   hForColor,
templateWindowSize, searchWindowSize)
        elif filter_name == "Anisotropic Diffusion":
            num_iterations,         kappa,         gamma,         option         =
self.get_diffusion_params(filter_params)
            return  self.anisotropic_diffusion(frame,  num_iterations,  kappa,  gamma,
option)
        elif filter_name == "Total Variation Denoising":
            weight, iterations = self.get_total_variation_params(filter_params)
            return self.total_variation_denoising(frame, weight, iterations)
        elif filter_name == "Wiener Filter":
            kernel_size, noise_var = self.get_wiener_filter_params(filter_params)
            print(kernel_size, noise_var)
            return self.wiener_filter(frame, kernel_size, noise_var)
        elif filter_name == "Adaptive Thresholding":
            block_size,     C,      adaptive_method,      threshold_type     =
self.get_adaptive_thresholding_params(filter_params)
            return   self.adaptive_threshold_each_channel(frame,   block_size,   C,
adaptive_method, threshold_type)
        elif filter_name == "Haar Wavelet Transform":
            wavelet, level, threshold = self.get_haar_wavelet_params(filter_params)
            return self.haar_wavelet_transform(frame, wavelet, level, threshold)
        elif filter_name == "Daubechies Wavelet Transform":
            return self.daubechies_wavelet_transform(frame)
        else:
            return frame  # Default: return original frame if filter not found
```

GENERATING POPUP WINDOW

The create_popup_window() method is designed to generate a pop-up window within a graphical user interface (GUI) application, displaying a cropped image alongside its histogram based on the selected image processing filter_name. It initializes a Toplevel window (self.popup_window) with a title that includes the filter name and a description indicating it displays the cropped image and its histogram. The window size is set to 1500x700 pixels to ensure ample space for image display and parameter adjustment widgets.

1. Parameter Widget Dictionary: Before proceeding with widget creation, the method initializes an empty dictionary self.parameter_widgets to store various parameter entry widgets dynamically created based on the selected filter.
2. Conditional Branching: The method employs conditional statements (if-elif) to determine the specific filter chosen (filter_name) and accordingly creates the necessary widgets for adjusting filter parameters.

3. Gaussian Filter: If the filter_name is "Gaussian", the method creates a frame (frame) within self.popup_window to organize parameter widgets. It adds Entry widgets for kernel_size and sigma, which control the size of the Gaussian kernel and its standard deviation, respectively.
4. Median Filter: For "Median" filtering, it creates an Entry widget for kernel_size directly in self.popup_window.
5. Mean Filter: Similarly, for "Mean" filtering, an Entry widget for kernel_size is placed directly within self.popup_window.
6. Bilateral Filtering: If the selected filter is "Bilateral Filtering", it organizes parameter widgets (Entry widgets for d, sigma_color, and sigma_space) within a frame (frame) to manage the spatial and color domain parameters of cv2.bilateralFilter.
7. Non-local Means Denoising: For "Non-local Means Denoising", it sets up parameter widgets (Entry widgets for h, hForColor, templateWindowSize, and searchWindowSize) in a frame (frame) to control the denoising effect applied by cv2.fastNlMeansDenoisingColored.
8. Anisotropic Diffusion: When "Anisotropic Diffusion" is selected, it creates parameter widgets (Entry widgets for num_iterations, kappa, gamma, and option) within a frame (frame) to adjust parameters for the anisotropic diffusion algorithm implemented in self.anisotropic_diffusion.
9. Total Variation Denoising: If "Total Variation Denoising" is chosen, the method sets up parameter widgets (Entry widgets for weight and iterations) in a frame (frame) to control the regularization and iterations applied in self.total_variation_denoising.
10. Buttons: Finally, the method adds Apply and Save buttons to button_frame at the bottom of self.popup_window. The Apply button (apply_button) is configured with a command that invokes an analysis method (self.analyze_histogram) to process the cropped image, while the Save button (save_button) triggers the self.save_filtered_image method to prompt the user to save the processed image to a specified file location.

By structuring the method in this manner, it facilitates dynamic creation of GUI elements tailored to each image processing filter, allowing users to interactively adjust parameters and observe the effects in real-time within the pop-up window. This approach enhances usability and functionality, enabling effective application of various filters and algorithms to enhance or transform images based on user preferences and requirements.

```python
    def create_popup_window(self, cropped_fram, filter_name):
        self.popup_window = tk.Toplevel(self.master)
        self.popup_window.title(filter_name + " --- Cropped Image and Its Histogram")
        self.popup_window.geometry("1500x700")

        # Create a dictionary to store filter parameter widgets
        self.parameter_widgets = {}

        if filter_name == "Gaussian":
            frame = tk.Frame(self.popup_window)
            frame.pack()

            label_kernel = tk.Label(frame, text="Kernel Size:")
            label_kernel.pack(side="left")
            self.kernel_gaussian = tk.Entry(frame)
            self.kernel_gaussian.insert(0, "5")  # Default value
            self.kernel_gaussian.pack(side="left")
            self.parameter_widgets["kernel_size_gaussian"] = self.kernel_gaussian

            label_sigma = tk.Label(frame, text="Sigma:")
            label_sigma.pack(side="left")
            self.sigma_gaussian = tk.Entry(frame)
            self.sigma_gaussian.insert(0, "1.0")  # Default value
            self.sigma_gaussian.pack(side="left")
            self.parameter_widgets["sigma_gaussian"] = self.sigma_gaussian

        elif filter_name == "Median":
            tk.Label(self.popup_window, text="Kernel Size:").pack()
            self.kernel_median= tk.Entry(self.popup_window)
            self.kernel_median.insert(0, "5")  # Default value
            self.kernel_median.pack()
            self.parameter_widgets["kernel_size_median"] = self.kernel_median

        elif filter_name == "Mean":
            tk.Label(self.popup_window, text="Kernel Size:").pack()
            self.kernel_mean= tk.Entry(self.popup_window)
            self.kernel_mean.insert(0, "5")  # Default value
            self.kernel_mean.pack()
            self.parameter_widgets["kernel_size_mean"] = self.kernel_mean

        elif filter_name == "Bilateral Filtering":
            frame = tk.Frame(self.popup_window)
            frame.pack()

            label_d = tk.Label(frame, text="D:")
            label_d.pack(side="left")
            self.d_bilateral = tk.Entry(frame)
            self.d_bilateral.insert(0, "9")  # Default value
            self.d_bilateral.pack(side="left")
            self.parameter_widgets["d_bilateral"] = self.d_bilateral

            label_sigma_color = tk.Label(frame, text="Sigma Color:")
            label_sigma_color.pack(side="left")
            self.sigma_color_bilateral = tk.Entry(frame)
            self.sigma_color_bilateral.insert(0, "75.0")  # Default value
            self.sigma_color_bilateral.pack(side="left")
            self.parameter_widgets["sigma_color_bilateral"] = self.sigma_color_bilateral
```

```python
            label_sigma_space = tk.Label(frame, text="Sigma Space:")
            label_sigma_space.pack(side="left")
            self.sigma_space_bilateral = tk.Entry(frame)
            self.sigma_space_bilateral.insert(0, "75.0")  # Default value
            self.sigma_space_bilateral.pack(side="left")
            self.parameter_widgets["sigma_space_bilateral"] = 
self.sigma_space_bilateral

        if filter_name == "Non-local Means Denoising":
            frame = tk.Frame(self.popup_window)
            frame.pack()

            label_h = tk.Label(frame, text="H:")
            label_h.pack(side="left")
            self.h_denoising = tk.Entry(frame)
            self.h_denoising.insert(0, "10")  # Default value
            self.h_denoising.pack(side="left")
            self.parameter_widgets["h_denoising"] = self.h_denoising

            label_hForColor = tk.Label(frame, text="HForColor:")
            label_hForColor.pack(side="left")
            self.hForColor_denoising = tk.Entry(frame)
            self.hForColor_denoising.insert(0, "10")  # Default value
            self.hForColor_denoising.pack(side="left")
            self.parameter_widgets["hForColor_denoising"] = self.hForColor_denoising

            label_templateWindowSize = tk.Label(frame, text="Template Window Size:")
            label_templateWindowSize.pack(side="left")
            self.templateWindowSize_denoising = tk.Entry(frame)
            self.templateWindowSize_denoising.insert(0, "7")  # Default value
            self.templateWindowSize_denoising.pack(side="left")
            self.parameter_widgets["templateWindowSize_denoising"] = 
self.templateWindowSize_denoising

            label_searchWindowSize = tk.Label(frame, text="Search Window Size:")
            label_searchWindowSize.pack(side="left")
            self.searchWindowSize_denoising = tk.Entry(frame)
            self.searchWindowSize_denoising.insert(0, "21")  # Default value
            self.searchWindowSize_denoising.pack(side="left")
            self.parameter_widgets["searchWindowSize_denoising"] = 
self.searchWindowSize_denoising

        if filter_name == "Anisotropic Diffusion":
            frame = tk.Frame(self.popup_window)
            frame.pack()

            label_num_iterations = tk.Label(frame, text="Number of Iterations:")
            label_num_iterations.pack(side="left")
            self.num_iterations_diffusion = tk.Entry(frame)
            self.num_iterations_diffusion.insert(0, "10")  # Default value
            self.num_iterations_diffusion.pack(side="left")
            self.parameter_widgets["num_iterations_diffusion"] = 
self.num_iterations_diffusion

            label_kappa = tk.Label(frame, text="Kappa:")
            label_kappa.pack(side="left")
            self.kappa_diffusion = tk.Entry(frame)
```

```python
            self.kappa_diffusion.insert(0, "15")  # Default value
            self.kappa_diffusion.pack(side="left")
            self.parameter_widgets["kappa_diffusion"] = self.kappa_diffusion

            label_gamma = tk.Label(frame, text="Gamma:")
            label_gamma.pack(side="left")
            self.gamma_diffusion = tk.Entry(frame)
            self.gamma_diffusion.insert(0, "0.2")  # Default value
            self.gamma_diffusion.pack(side="left")
            self.parameter_widgets["gamma_diffusion"] = self.gamma_diffusion

            label_option = tk.Label(frame, text="Option:")
            label_option.pack(side="left")
            self.option_diffusion = tk.Entry(frame)
            self.option_diffusion.insert(0, "1")  # Default value
            self.option_diffusion.pack(side="left")
            self.parameter_widgets["option_diffusion"] = self.option_diffusion

        if filter_name == "Total Variation Denoising":
            frame = tk.Frame(self.popup_window)
            frame.pack()

            label_weight = tk.Label(frame, text="Weight:")
            label_weight.pack(side="left")
            self.weight_denoising = tk.Entry(frame)
            self.weight_denoising.insert(0, "0.01")  # Default value
            self.weight_denoising.pack(side="left")
            self.parameter_widgets["weight_denoising"] = self.weight_denoising

            label_iterations = tk.Label(frame, text="Iterations:")
            label_iterations.pack(side="left")
            self.iterations_denoising = tk.Entry(frame)
            self.iterations_denoising.insert(0, "20")  # Default value
            self.iterations_denoising.pack(side="left")
            self.parameter_widgets["iterations_denoising"] = self.iterations_denoising

        if filter_name == "Haar Wavelet Transform":
            frame = tk.Frame(self.popup_window)
            frame.pack()

            label_wavelet = tk.Label(frame, text="Wavelet Type:")
            label_wavelet.pack(side="left")
            self.wavelet_type = tk.Entry(frame)
            self.wavelet_type.insert(0, "haar")  # Default value
            self.wavelet_type.pack(side="left")
            self.parameter_widgets["wavelet_type"] = self.wavelet_type

            label_level = tk.Label(frame, text="Decomposition Level:")
            label_level.pack(side="left")
            self.wavelet_level = tk.Entry(frame)
            self.wavelet_level.insert(0, "1")  # Default value
            self.wavelet_level.pack(side="left")
            self.parameter_widgets["wavelet_level"] = self.wavelet_level

            label_threshold = tk.Label(frame, text="Threshold:")
            label_threshold.pack(side="left")
            self.threshold = tk.Entry(frame)
            self.threshold.insert(0, "0.1")  # Default value
```

```python
            self.threshold.pack(side="left")
            self.parameter_widgets["threshold"] = self.threshold

        if filter_name == "Adaptive Thresholding":
            frame = tk.Frame(self.popup_window)
            frame.pack()

            label_block_size = tk.Label(frame, text="Block Size:")
            label_block_size.pack(side="left")
            self.block_size_entry = tk.Entry(frame)
            self.block_size_entry.insert(0, "11")  # Default value
            self.block_size_entry.pack(side="left")
            self.parameter_widgets["block_size"] = self.block_size_entry

            label_c = tk.Label(frame, text="C:")
            label_c.pack(side="left")
            self.c_entry = tk.Entry(frame)
            self.c_entry.insert(0, "2")  # Default value
            self.c_entry.pack(side="left")
            self.parameter_widgets["c"] = self.c_entry

            label_adaptive_method = tk.Label(frame, text="Adaptive Method:")
            label_adaptive_method.pack(side="left")
            self.adaptive_method_entry = ttk.Combobox(frame, values=[cv2.ADAPTIVE_THRESH_MEAN_C, cv2.ADAPTIVE_THRESH_GAUSSIAN_C])
            self.adaptive_method_entry.insert(0, cv2.ADAPTIVE_THRESH_MEAN_C)  # Default value
            self.adaptive_method_entry.pack(side="left")
            self.parameter_widgets["adaptive_method"] = self.adaptive_method_entry

            label_threshold_type = tk.Label(frame, text="Threshold Type:")
            label_threshold_type.pack(side="left")
            self.threshold_type_entry = ttk.Combobox(frame, values=[cv2.THRESH_BINARY, cv2.THRESH_BINARY_INV])
            self.threshold_type_entry.insert(0, cv2.THRESH_BINARY)  # Default value
            self.threshold_type_entry.pack(side="left")
            self.parameter_widgets["threshold_type"] = self.threshold_type_entry

        if filter_name == "Wiener Filter":
            frame = tk.Frame(self.popup_window)
            frame.pack()

            label_kernel_size = tk.Label(frame, text="Kernel Size:")
            label_kernel_size.pack(side="left")
            self.kernel_size_entry = tk.Entry(frame)
            self.kernel_size_entry.insert(0, "5")  # Default value
            self.kernel_size_entry.pack(side="left")
            self.parameter_widgets["kernel_size"] = self.kernel_size_entry

            label_noise_var = tk.Label(frame, text="Noise Variance:")
            label_noise_var.pack(side="left")
            self.noise_var_entry = tk.Entry(frame)
            self.noise_var_entry.insert(0, "0.01")  # Default value
            self.noise_var_entry.pack(side="left")
            self.parameter_widgets["noise_var"] = self.noise_var_entry

        # Frame for Apply and Save buttons
        button_frame = tk.Frame(self.popup_window)
```

```
        button_frame.pack()
        
        # Add an Apply button to apply the filter
        apply_button        =        tk.Button(button_frame,        text="Apply", 
command=lambda:self.analyze_histogram("OLD"))
        apply_button.pack(side="left")
        
        # Add a Save button to save the filtered image
        save_button         =        tk.Button(button_frame,         text="Save", 
command=self.save_filtered_image)
        save_button.pack(side="left")
        
    def save_filtered_image(self):
        # Ask the user for a location and filename to save the image
        file_path       =       filedialog.asksaveasfilename(defaultextension=".png", 
filetypes=[("PNG files", "*.png"), ("JPEG files", "*.jpg"), ("All files", "*.*")])
        
        if file_path and self.cropped_img is not None:
            # Ensure self.cropped_img is a valid numpy array and convert to RGB
            cropped_img_array = np.array(self.cropped_img)
            cropped_img_rgb = cv2.cvtColor(cropped_img_array, cv2.COLOR_BGR2RGB)
            cv2.imwrite(file_path, cropped_img_rgb)
```

RUNNING DESCRIPTOR BASED IMAGES MATCHING

run_outside_script() Method

- The run_outside_script method is designed to execute an external Python script from within another Python program. Here's a breakdown of its functionality:
- Absolute Script Path: It first retrieves the directory path of the current script using os.path.abspath(__file__), which provides the absolute path of the current Python file. This ensures that the method knows where to locate the external scripts.
- Script Path Construction: It constructs the absolute path to the external script by joining the script directory path (script_directory) with the filename (file_name) provided as an argument to the method using os.path.join().
- Path Debugging: For debugging purposes, it prints out the absolute path of the external script using print(f"Absolute script path: {script_path}").
- File Existence Check: It checks if the script file exists at the constructed script_path using os.path.exists(). If the file does not exist, it prints an error message indicating that the file was not found and returns from the method early.
- Executing the Script: If the script file exists, it proceeds to execute it using subprocess.Popen(). This function launches a new process and specifies "python" as the command to invoke Python interpreter, with script_path as an argument.

- Waiting for Completion: It calls process.communicate() to wait for the external script process to finish execution before proceeding. This ensures that the method waits until the script completes its task before continuing.
- Success Message: Upon successful execution of the script, it prints a message indicating that the script executed successfully using print("Script executed successfully.").
- Exception Handling: The method is wrapped in a try-except block to catch any exceptions that may occur during script execution. If an exception is raised (Exception as e), it catches the exception and prints an error message detailing the nature of the exception using print(f"An error occurred while running the script: {e}").

choose_matcher() Method

The choose_matcher() method is responsible for determining which feature matching algorithm to use based on user selection from a combobox (self.matcher_combobox). Here's how it operates:

- Selected Matcher: It retrieves the currently selected matcher algorithm from the combobox using self.matcher_combobox.get() and assigns it to selected_matcher.
- Conditional Branching: Using an if-elif structure, it checks the value of selected_matcher to determine which external script to run for performing the matching:
    - If selected_matcher is "SIFT", it calls self.run_outside_script("SIFTMatcher_NEW.py").
    - If selected_matcher is "ORB", it calls self.run_outside_script("ORBMacher.py").
    - Similarly, it handles other matcher algorithms like "FAST", "AGAST", "BRISK", and "AKAZE" by invoking self.run_outside_script() with the corresponding script filename.
- Execution Flow: Depending on the selected matcher, choose_matcher delegates the task of executing the corresponding external script to run_outside_script(), ensuring modularity and separation of concerns.
- Integration with GUI: This method is typically bound to an event handler in a GUI application, allowing users to select different matching algorithms dynamically and trigger their execution by interacting with the combobox.

- Error Handling: Since choose_matcher indirectly calls run_outside_script, it inherits the exception handling from run_outside_script. Any errors encountered during script execution will be caught by run_outside_script and printed as an error message.
- Functionality Expansion: If additional matching algorithms are added in the future, they can be seamlessly integrated into choose_matcher by adding new elif conditions, thereby enhancing the application's flexibility and functionality.

By organizing the code in this structured manner, the methods facilitate the execution of external scripts based on user selection and provide robust error handling to manage potential issues during script execution. This approach ensures smooth integration of external functionalities within the Python application while maintaining clarity and maintainability.

```python
def run_outside_script(self, file_name):
    try:
        # Get the absolute path of the external script
        script_directory = os.path.dirname(os.path.abspath(__file__))
        script_path = os.path.join(script_directory, file_name)

        # Print the path for debugging
        print(f"Absolute script path: {script_path}")

        if not os.path.exists(script_path):
            print(f"File {script_path} not found.")
            return

        # Call the external script using the absolute path
        process = subprocess.Popen(["python", script_path], shell=True)
        process.communicate()  # Wait for the process to finish
        print("Script executed successfully.")

    except Exception as e:
        print(f"An error occurred while running the script: {e}")

def choose_matcher(self):
    selected_matcher = self.matcher_combobox.get()
    if selected_matcher == "SIFT":
        self.run_outside_script("SIFTMacher_NEW.py")
    elif selected_matcher == "ORB":
        self.run_outside_script("ORBMacher.py")
    elif selected_matcher == "FAST":
        self.run_outside_script("FASTMatcher.py")
    elif selected_matcher == "AGAST":
        self.run_outside_script("AGASTMatcher.py")
    elif selected_matcher == "BRISK":
        self.run_outside_script("BRISKMatcher.py")
    elif selected_matcher == "AKAZE":
        self.run_outside_script("AKAZEMatcher.py")
```

ENTRY POINT

```
def main():
    root = tk.Tk()
    app = Filter_CroppedFrame(root)
    root.mainloop()

if __name__ == "__main__":
    main()
```

RUNNING PROGRAM

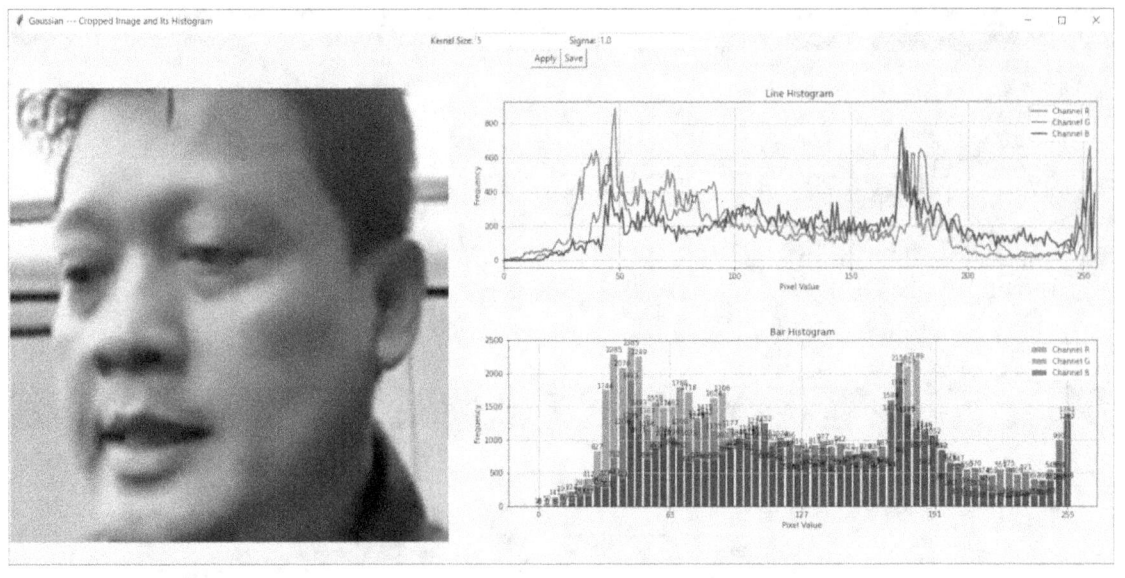

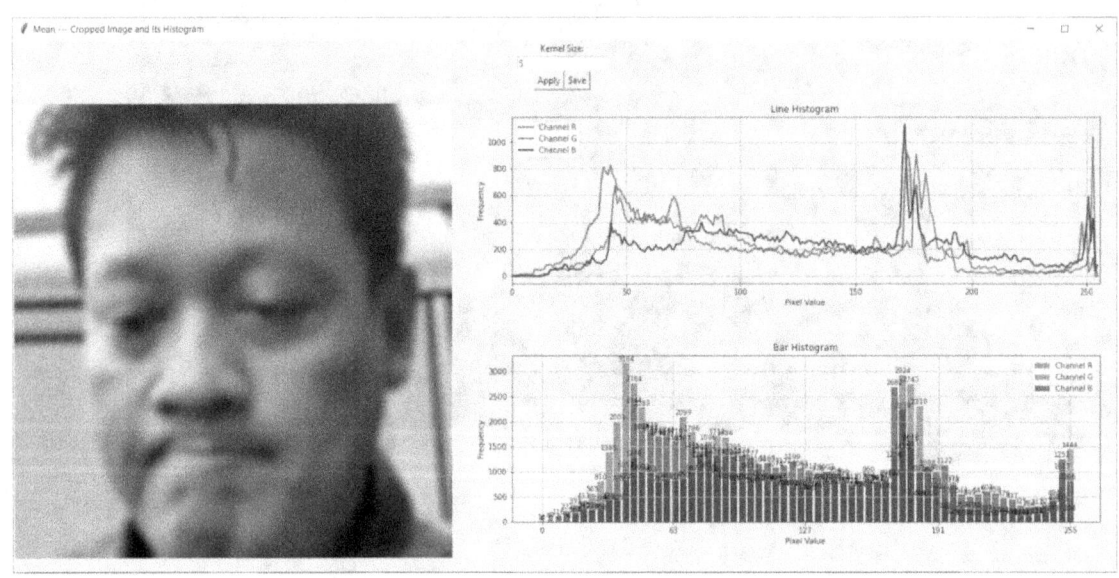

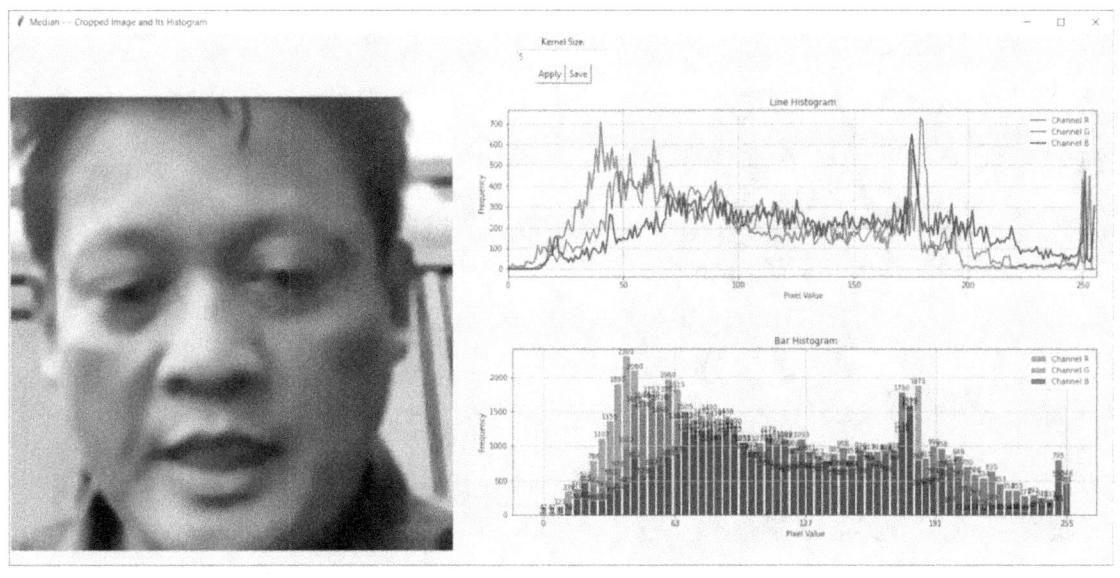
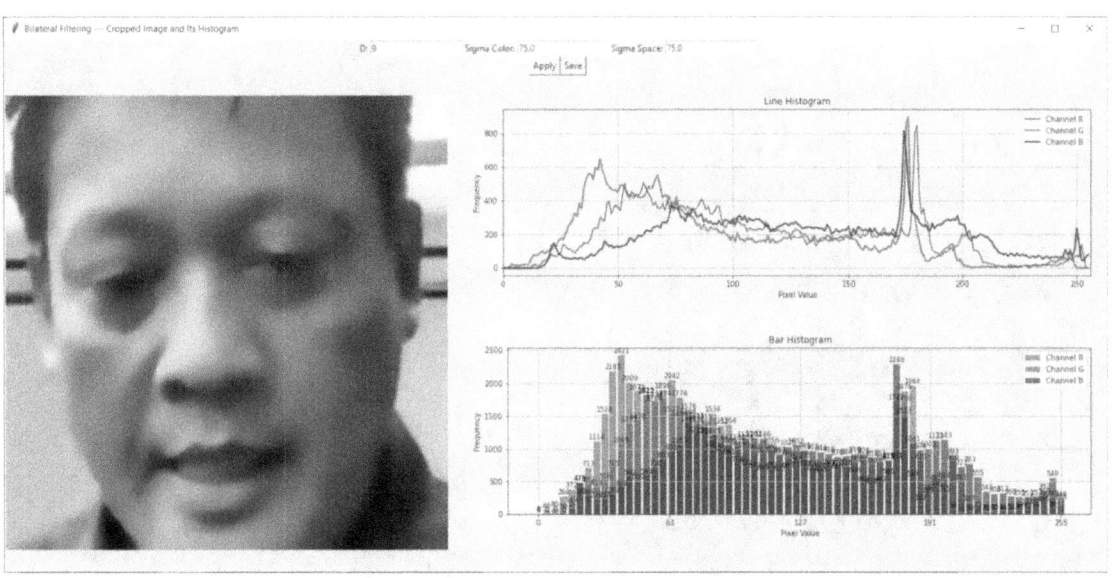

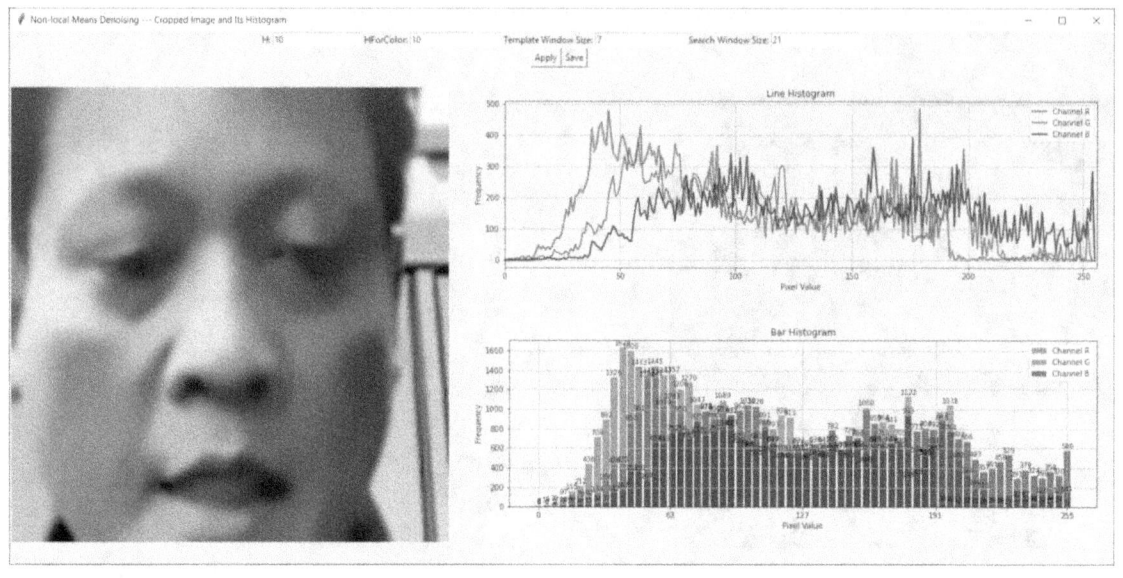

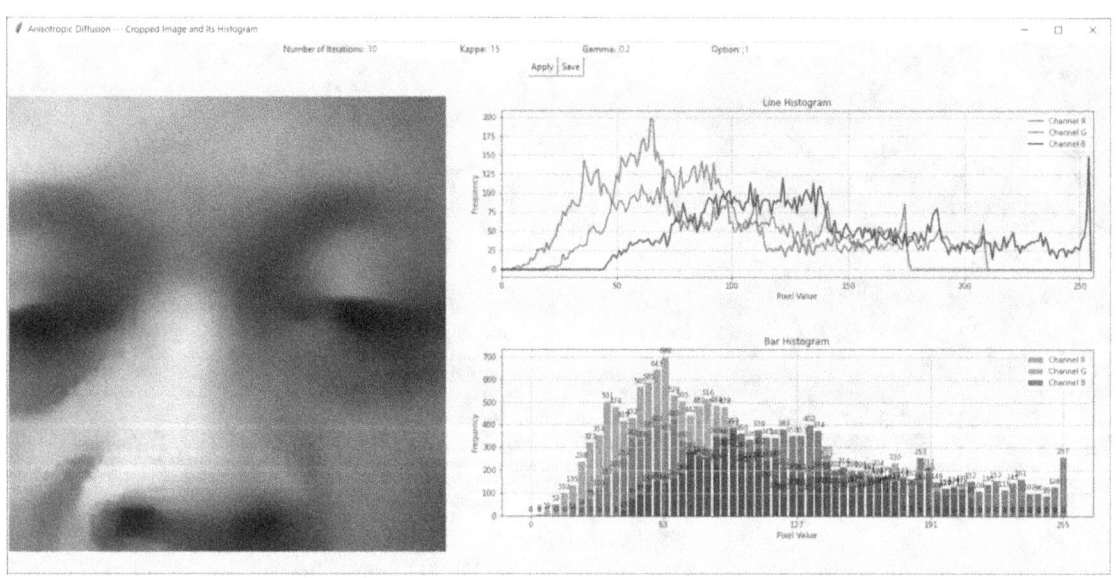

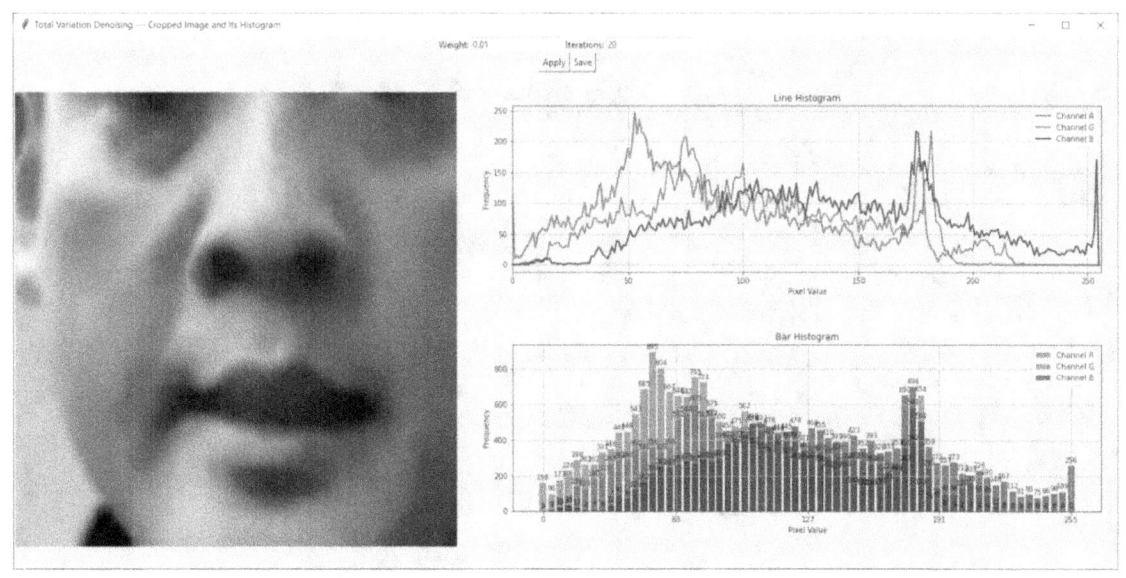

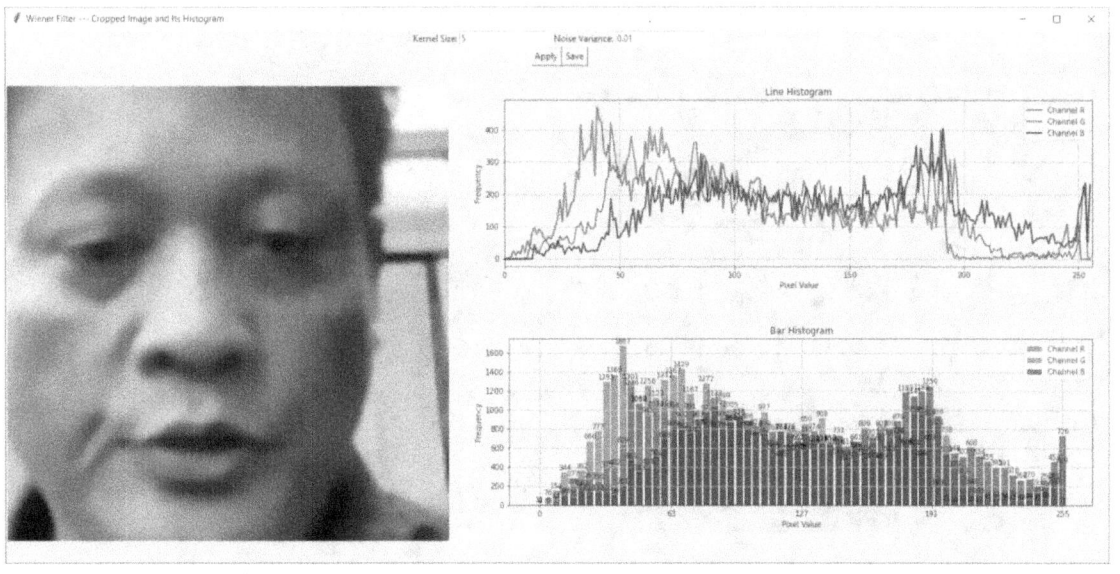

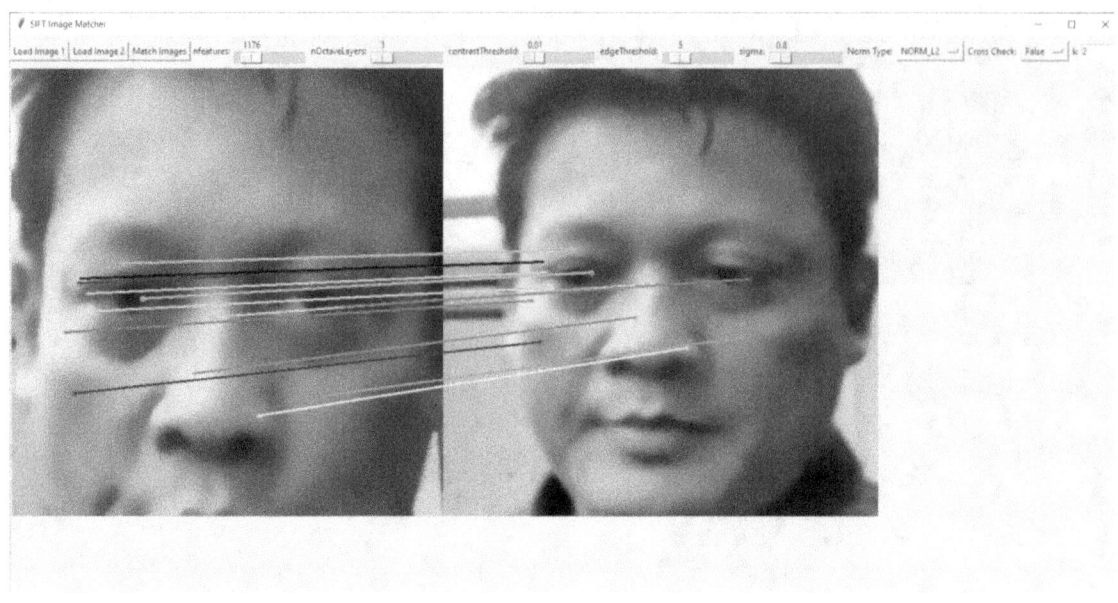

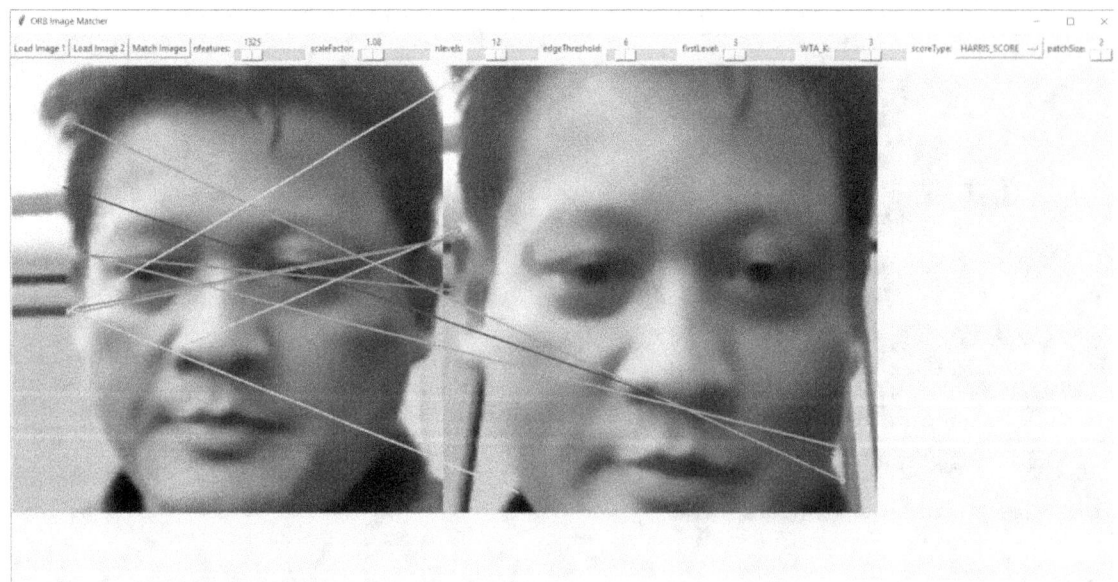

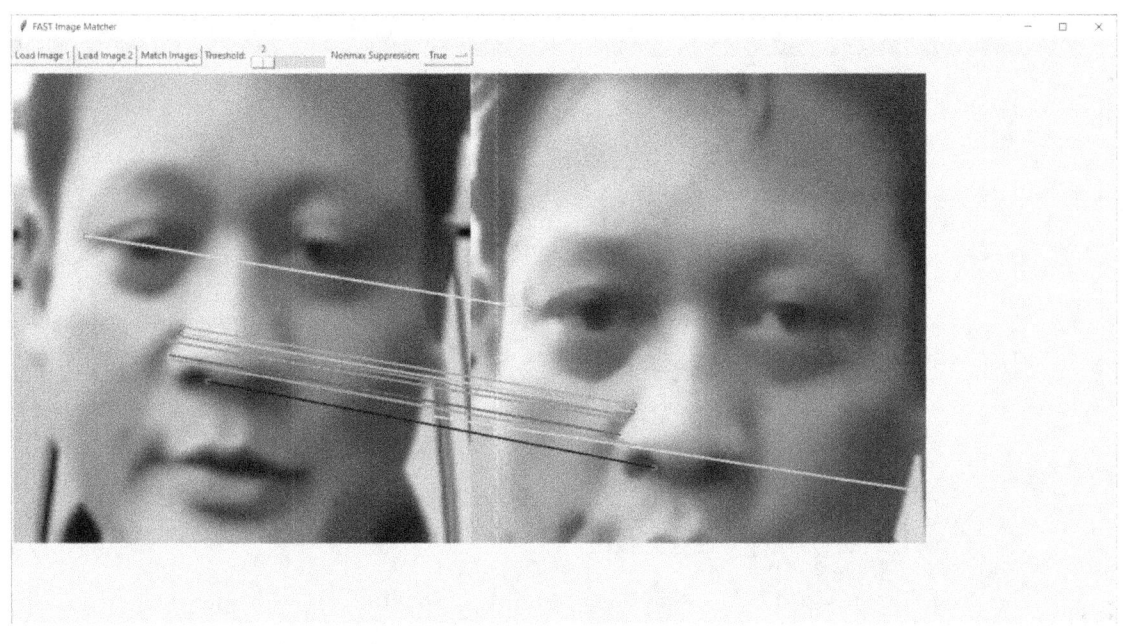

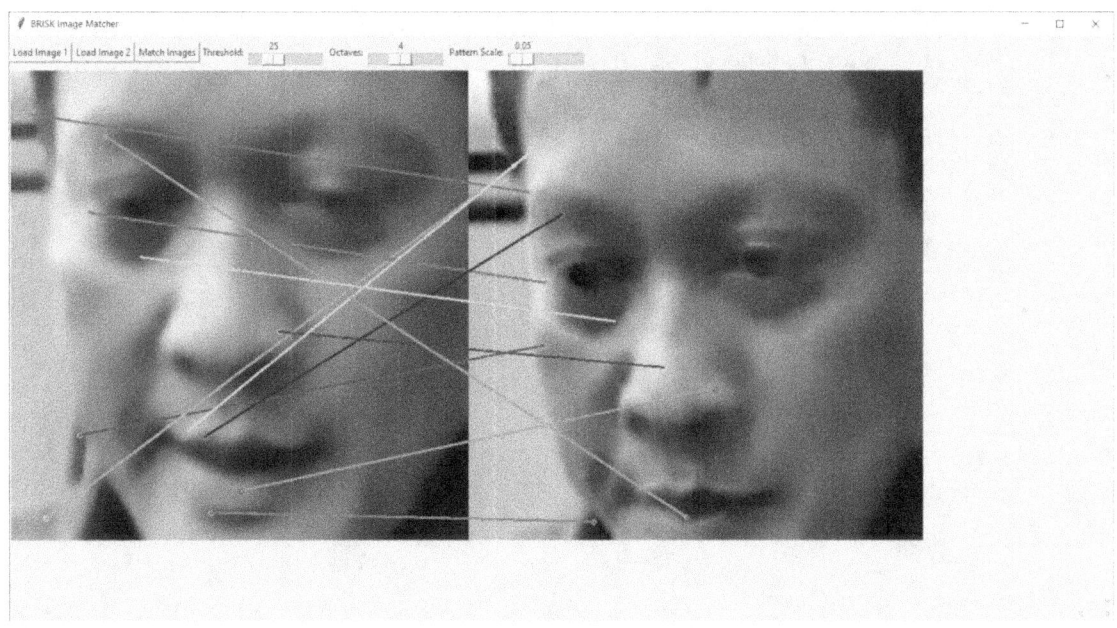

SOURCE CODE

```python
#rgb_cropped_filtered_frame_object__matching.py
import tkinter as tk
from tkinter import ttk
from tkinter import filedialog
from PIL import Image, ImageTk
import imageio
import pywt
import cv2
import numpy as np
import matplotlib.pyplot as plt
import subprocess
import os

class Filter_CroppedFrame:
    def __init__(self, master):
        self.master = master
        self.master.title("Object Matching Video")
        self.file_name = ""
        self.set_window_title()  # Set window title initially

        self.frame_number_label = tk.Label(master, text="Frame: 0")
        self.frame_number_label.pack()

        self.video = None
        self.video_path = None
        self.paused = False
        self.zoom_scale = tk.IntVar(value=1)
        self.frame_index = 0
        self.bbox = None
        self.bbox_rect = None  # Initialize bbox_rect attribute to None

        # Available filters
        self.filters = ["None", "Gaussian", "Mean", "Median", "Bilateral Filtering",
                        "Non-local Means Denoising", "Anisotropic Diffusion",
                        "Total Variation Denoising", "Wiener Filter",
                        "Adaptive Thresholding", "Haar Wavelet Transform",
                        "Daubechies Wavelet Transform", "SRCNN Super Resolution",
                        "EDSR Super Resolution"]

        # Available matchers
        self.matchers = ["SIFT", "ORB", "FAST", "AGAST", "BRISK", "AKAZE"]

        self.create_widgets()

    def create_widgets(self):
        # Panel for control buttons
        control_panel = tk.Frame(self.master)
        control_panel.pack(padx=10, pady=(0, 10), fill="x")

        # Button to open a video file
        self.open_button = tk.Button(control_panel, text="Open Video", command=self.open_video)
        self.open_button.grid(row=0, column=0, padx=10, pady=5)
```

```python
        # Combobox for selecting zoom scale
        self.zoom_combobox = ttk.Combobox(control_panel, textvariable=self.zoom_scale, values=list(range(1, 11)))
        self.zoom_combobox.grid(row=0, column=1, padx=10, pady=5)
        self.zoom_combobox.bind("<<ComboboxSelected>>", self.update_zoom)

        # Button to play/pause the video
        self.play_button = tk.Button(control_panel, text="Play/Pause", command=self.toggle_play_pause)
        self.play_button.grid(row=0, column=2, padx=10, pady=5)

        # Button to stop the video
        self.stop_button = tk.Button(control_panel, text="Stop", command=self.stop_video)
        self.stop_button.grid(row=0, column=3, padx=10, pady=5)

        # Button to navigate to the previous frame
        self.prev_frame_button = tk.Button(control_panel, text="Previous Frame", command=self.prev_frame)
        self.prev_frame_button.grid(row=0, column=4, padx=10, pady=5)

        # Button to navigate to the next frame
        self.next_frame_button = tk.Button(control_panel, text="Next Frame", command=self.next_frame)
        self.next_frame_button.grid(row=0, column=5, padx=10, pady=5)

        # Button to open new instance
        self.open_new_instance_button = tk.Button(control_panel, text="Open New Instance", command=self.open_new_instance)
        self.open_new_instance_button.grid(row=0, column=6, padx=10, pady=5)

        # Label for the selecting filters
        self.matcher_label = tk.Label(control_panel, text="Select Filter:")
        self.matcher_label.grid(row=0, column=7, padx=10, pady=5, sticky="e")

        # Combobox for selecting filters
        self.filter_combobox = ttk.Combobox(control_panel, values=self.filters)
        self.filter_combobox.grid(row=0, column=8, padx=10, pady=5)
        self.filter_combobox.current(0)  # Set default value

        # Label for the selecting matchers
        self.matcher_label = tk.Label(control_panel, text="Select Matcher:")
        self.matcher_label.grid(row=0, column=9, padx=10, pady=5, sticky="e")

        # Combobox for selecting matchers
        self.matcher_combobox = ttk.Combobox(control_panel, values=self.matchers)
        self.matcher_combobox.grid(row=0, column=10, padx=10, pady=5)
        self.matcher_combobox.current(0)  # Set default value
        self.matcher_combobox.bind("<<ComboboxSelected>>", lambda event: self.choose_matcher())

        # Panel for video display
        video_panel = tk.Frame(self.master)
        video_panel.pack(padx=10, pady=10)

        # Canvas to display the original video
        canvas_width = 1400
        canvas_height = 650
```

```
        self.canvas = tk.Canvas(video_panel, width=canvas_width, height=canvas_height)
        self.canvas.pack(side="left", fill="both", expand=True)
        self.canvas.bind("<MouseWheel>", self.on_mousewheel)
        self.canvas.bind("<ButtonPress-1>", self.on_press)
        self.canvas.bind("<B1-Motion>", self.on_drag)
        self.canvas.bind("<ButtonRelease-1>", self.on_release)   # Bind ButtonRelease event

        self.scrollbar_vertical = tk.Scrollbar(video_panel, orient="vertical", command=self.canvas.yview)
        self.scrollbar_vertical.pack(side="right", fill="y")

        self.scrollbar_horizontal = tk.Scrollbar(self.master, orient="horizontal", command=self.canvas.xview)
        self.scrollbar_horizontal.pack(side="bottom", fill="x")
        #self.canvas.configure(yscrollcommand=self.scrollbar_vertical.set, xscrollcommand=self.scrollbar_horizontal.set)

    def open_video(self):
        self.video_path = filedialog.askopenfilename(filetypes=[("Video files", "*.mp4;*.avi;*.mkv;*.wmv")])
        if self.video_path:
            self.video = imageio.get_reader(self.video_path)
            self.file_name = self.video_path.split('/')[-1]
            self.set_window_title()
            self.number_of_frames = self.video.count_frames()
            self.play_video()  # Auto-play the video when opened
            self.show_frame()  # Show the first frame when the video is opened

    def play_video(self):
        if self.video:
            self.paused = False
            self.show_frame()

    def toggle_play_pause(self):
        if self.video:
            self.paused = not self.paused
            if not self.paused:
                self.play_video()  # If not paused, start playing

    def stop_video(self):
        self.paused = True
        self.frame_index = 0
        self.bbox = None
        self.show_frame()

    def update_zoom(self, event=None):
        self.show_frame()

    def show_frame(self, auto_play=True):
        if self.video:
            if not self.paused or not auto_play:
                if 0 <= self.frame_index < self.number_of_frames:
                    frame = self.video.get_data(self.frame_index)
                    frame = cv2.cvtColor(frame, cv2.COLOR_RGB2BGR)

                    # Get the zoom scale value
                    zoom_value = self.zoom_scale.get()
```

```python
                        height, width = frame.shape[:2]
                        frame = cv2.resize(frame, (int(width * zoom_value), int(height * zoom_value)))

                        frame = cv2.cvtColor(frame, cv2.COLOR_BGR2RGB)
                        frame = Image.fromarray(frame)
                        photo = ImageTk.PhotoImage(frame)
                        self.photo = photo
                        self.canvas.delete("video")
                        self.canvas.create_image(0, 0, anchor="nw", image=photo, tags="video")

                        self.frame_number_label.config(text=f"Frame: {self.frame_index} / {self.number_of_frames}", font=("Helvetica", 18))

                        # Adjust the scroll region to the new image size
                        self.canvas.config(scrollregion=self.canvas.bbox("all"))

                        if auto_play:
                            self.frame_index += 1
                            self.master.after(30, self.show_frame)

    def prev_frame(self):
        if self.frame_index > 0:
            self.frame_index -= 1
            self.show_frame(auto_play=False)

    def next_frame(self):
        if self.video and self.frame_index < self.number_of_frames - 1:
            self.frame_index += 1
            self.show_frame(auto_play=False)

    def on_mousewheel(self, event):
        direction = event.delta // 120
        current_value = int(self.zoom_scale.get())
        if direction == 1 and current_value < 10:
            current_value += 1
        elif direction == -1 and current_value > 1:
            current_value -= 1
        self.zoom_scale.set(current_value)
        self.update_zoom()

    def on_press(self, event):
        self.start_x = self.canvas.canvasx(event.x)
        self.start_y = self.canvas.canvasy(event.y)
        self.bbox = None

    def on_drag(self, event):
        cur_x = self.canvas.canvasx(event.x)
        cur_y = self.canvas.canvasy(event.y)
        if self.bbox_rect:
            self.canvas.delete(self.bbox_rect)
        self.bbox = (self.start_x, self.start_y, cur_x, cur_y)
        self.bbox_rect = self.canvas.create_rectangle(*self.bbox, outline='#fc3d3d', width=5)

    def on_release(self, event):
```

```python
            self.analyze_histogram("NEW")  # Call analyze_histogram() method when the mouse button is released

    def set_window_title(self):
        if self.file_name:
            self.master.title(f"Analyzing RGB Histogram of Frame - {self.file_name}")
            self.master.title_font = ("Helvetica", 16, "bold")
        else:
            self.master.title("Analyzing RGB Histogram of Frame")

    def analyze_histogram(self, state):
        if self.bbox is None:
            return

        x1, y1, x2, y2 = [int(self.canvas.canvasx(coord)) for coord in self.bbox]
        if x1 < x2 and y1 < y2:
            pass
        elif x1 > x2 and y1 > y2:
            x1, x2 = x2, x1
            y1, y2 = y2, y1
        elif x1 > x2 and y1 < y2:
            x1, x2 = x2, x1
        elif x1 < x2 and y1 > y2:
            y1, y2 = y2, y1

        zoom_value = self.zoom_scale.get()
        x1 //= zoom_value
        y1 //= zoom_value
        x2 //= zoom_value
        y2 //= zoom_value

        frame = self.video.get_data(self.frame_index)
        frame = cv2.cvtColor(frame, cv2.COLOR_RGB2BGR)

        if x1 < x2 and y1 < y2:
            cropped_frame = frame[y1:y2, x1:x2]
        else:
            return

        selected_filter = self.update_filter_params(state)

        # Apply selected filter
        self.filtered_frame =  self.apply_filter(selected_filter,  cropped_frame, self.filter_params)

        self.create_popup_window(self.filtered_frame, selected_filter)
        self.display_cropped_image(self.filtered_frame)
        self.display_histograms(self.filtered_frame)

    def display_cropped_image(self, cropped_frame):
        if cropped_frame is None:
            print("Error: Cropped frame is None.")
            return

        if cropped_frame.size == 0:
            print("Error: Cropped frame is empty.")
            return
```

```python
        cropped_frame_frame = tk.Frame(self.popup_window)
        cropped_frame_frame.pack(side="left")

        # Ensure that the super-resolved image is in RGB format
        cropped_frame_rgb = cv2.cvtColor(cropped_frame, cv2.COLOR_BGR2RGB)

        cropped_img = Image.fromarray(cropped_frame_rgb)
        self.cropped_img = cropped_img.resize((600, 600))

        cropped_photo = ImageTk.PhotoImage(self.cropped_img)
        cropped_canvas = tk.Canvas(cropped_frame_frame, width=600, height=600)
        cropped_canvas.pack(side="left", anchor="nw")
        cropped_canvas.create_image(0, 0, anchor="nw", image=cropped_photo)
        cropped_canvas.image = cropped_photo

    def display_histograms(self, cropped_frame):
        histograms_frame = tk.Frame(self.popup_window)
        histograms_frame.pack(side="right", padx=20)

        self.display_line_histogram(cropped_frame, histograms_frame)
        self.display_bar_histogram(cropped_frame, histograms_frame)

    def display_line_histogram(self, cropped_frame, histograms_frame):
        # clears widget
        for widget in histograms_frame.winfo_children():
            widget.destroy()

        line_histogram_frame = tk.Frame(histograms_frame)
        line_histogram_frame.pack(side="top", pady=5)

        # Set the background color to a control-like color (light gray)
        control_bg_color = '#f0f0f0'

        fig, ax = plt.subplots(figsize=(12, 4), facecolor=control_bg_color)
        ax.set_facecolor(control_bg_color)

        color = ('r', 'g', 'b')
        for i, col in enumerate(color):
            histr = cv2.calcHist([cropped_frame], [i], None, [256], [0, 256])
            plt.plot(histr, color=col, label=f'Channel {col.upper()}', linewidth=2)
            plt.xlim([0, 256])
        plt.title('Line Histogram')
        plt.xlabel('Pixel Value')
        plt.ylabel('Frequency')
        plt.tight_layout()
        plt.grid(True)
        plt.legend()

        line_histogram_img = self.plot_to_image(plt)
        self.display_histogram_image(line_histogram_frame, line_histogram_img)

    def display_bar_histogram(self, cropped_frame, histograms_frame):
        bar_histogram_frame = tk.Frame(histograms_frame)
        bar_histogram_frame.pack(side="bottom", pady=5)

        # Set the background color to a control-like color (light gray)
        control_bg_color = '#f0f0f0'
```

```python
        # Create the figure and axes with the specified background color
        fig, ax = plt.subplots(figsize=(12, 4), facecolor=control_bg_color)
        ax.set_facecolor(control_bg_color)

        color = ('r', 'g', 'b')
        num_bars = 64
        for i, col in enumerate(color):
            hist_range = (0, 256)
            hist_counts, _ = np.histogram(cropped_frame[:, :, i], bins=num_bars, range=hist_range)
            ax.bar(np.arange(num_bars), hist_counts, color=col, alpha=0.7, label=f'Channel {col.upper()}')
            for index, value in enumerate(hist_counts):
                ax.text(index, value + 10, str(int(value)), ha='center', va='bottom', fontsize=9)

        ax.set_title('Bar Histogram')
        ax.set_xlabel('Pixel Value')
        ax.set_ylabel('Frequency')
        ax.set_xticks(np.linspace(0, num_bars-1, num=5))
        ax.set_xticklabels(np.linspace(0, 255, num=5, dtype=int))  # Adjust x-axis ticks
        ax.grid(True)
        ax.legend()
        plt.tight_layout()

        bar_histogram_img = self.plot_to_image(fig)
        self.display_histogram_image(bar_histogram_frame, bar_histogram_img)

    def display_histogram_image(self, parent_frame, img):
        histogram_photo = ImageTk.PhotoImage(image=img)
        histogram_canvas = tk.Canvas(parent_frame, width=900, height=300)
        histogram_canvas.pack(side="bottom", anchor="se")
        histogram_canvas.create_image(0, 0, anchor="nw", image=histogram_photo)
        histogram_canvas.image = histogram_photo

    def plot_histogram_bar_to_image(self, image):
        # Calculate histogram for each channel
        histograms = []
        for i in range(3):
            hist_range = (0, 256)
            hist_counts, _ = np.histogram(image[:, :, i], bins=64, range=hist_range)  # Adjust bins to 64
            histograms.append(hist_counts)

        # Extracting only 64 bins from the histogram
        num_bins = 64  # Adjusted to 64 bins

        # Generating colors for each channel
        colors = ['red', 'green', 'blue']

        plt.figure()
        for i, histogram in enumerate(histograms):
            # Normalize the histogram counts for better visualization
            hist_counts = histogram / np.sum(histogram)
            # Setting the color for each channel
            plt.bar(np.arange(num_bins), hist_counts[:num_bins], color=colors[i], alpha=0.7, label=f'Channel {["Red", "Green", "Blue"][i]}')
```

```python
        plt.xlabel('Pixel Value')
        plt.ylabel('Normalized Frequency')
        plt.title('RGB Channel Histograms')
        plt.grid(True)
        plt.tight_layout()
        plt.legend()

        # Convert the histogram bar graph to an image
        histogram_bar_img = self.plot_to_image(plt)
        histogram_bar_photo = ImageTk.PhotoImage(image=histogram_bar_img)

        return histogram_bar_photo

    def plot_to_image(self, plt):
        plt.savefig('temp_plot.png')
        img = Image.open('temp_plot.png')
        return img

    def update_filter_params(self, state):
        # Get selected filter from combobox
        selected_filter = self.filter_combobox.get()
        self.filter_params = {}
        if state != "NEW" and selected_filter=="Gaussian":
            self.kernel_gaussian_val = int(self.parameter_widgets["kernel_size_gaussian"].get())
            self.sigma_gaussian_val = float(self.parameter_widgets["sigma_gaussian"].get())

            # Define filter parameters as a dictionary
            self.filter_params = {"kernel_size_gaussian": self.kernel_gaussian_val, "sigma_gaussian": self.sigma_gaussian_val}

            # Updates Gaussian Filter Params
            self.kernel_gaussian.delete(0, tk.END)
            self.sigma_gaussian.delete(0, tk.END)
            self.kernel_gaussian.insert(0, str(self.kernel_gaussian_val))
            self.sigma_gaussian.insert(0, str(self.sigma_gaussian_val))

        if state != "NEW" and selected_filter=="Median":
            self.kernel_median_val = int(self.parameter_widgets["kernel_size_median"].get())
            # Define filter parameters as a dictionary
            self.filter_params = {"kernel_size_median": self.kernel_median_val}

            #Median Filter Param
            self.kernel_median.delete(0, tk.END)
            self.kernel_median.insert(0, str(self.kernel_median_val))

        if state != "NEW" and selected_filter=="Mean":
            self.kernel_mean_val = int(self.parameter_widgets["kernel_size_mean"].get())
            # Define filter parameters as a dictionary
            self.filter_params = {"kernel_size_mean": self.kernel_mean_val}

            #Mean Filter Param
            self.kernel_mean.delete(0, tk.END)
            self.kernel_mean.insert(0, str(self.kernel_mean_val))
```

```python
        if state != "NEW" and selected_filter == "Bilateral Filtering":
            # Get the parameter values from the corresponding widgets
            d = int(self.parameter_widgets["d_bilateral"].get())
            sigma_color = float(self.parameter_widgets["sigma_color_bilateral"].get())
            sigma_space = float(self.parameter_widgets["sigma_space_bilateral"].get())

            # Define filter parameters as a dictionary
            self.filter_params = {"d_bilateral": d, "sigma_color_bilateral": sigma_color, "sigma_space_bilateral": sigma_space}

            # Updates Bilateral Filter Params
            self.d_bilateral.delete(0, tk.END)
            self.sigma_color_bilateral.delete(0, tk.END)
            self.sigma_space_bilateral.delete(0, tk.END)
            self.d_bilateral.insert(0, str(d))
            self.sigma_color_bilateral.insert(0, str(sigma_color))
            self.sigma_space_bilateral.insert(0, str(sigma_space))

        if state != "NEW" and selected_filter == "Non-local Means Denoising":
            self.h_val = float(self.parameter_widgets["h_denoising"].get())
            self.hForColor_val = float(self.parameter_widgets["hForColor_denoising"].get())
            self.templateWindowSize_val = int(self.parameter_widgets["templateWindowSize_denoising"].get())
            self.searchWindowSize_val = int(self.parameter_widgets["searchWindowSize_denoising"].get())

            # Define filter parameters as a dictionary
            self.filter_params = {
                "h": self.h_val,
                "hForColor": self.hForColor_val,
                "templateWindowSize": self.templateWindowSize_val,
                "searchWindowSize": self.searchWindowSize_val
            }

            # Update filter params in the GUI
            self.parameter_widgets["h_denoising"].delete(0, tk.END)
            self.parameter_widgets["hForColor_denoising"].delete(0, tk.END)
            self.parameter_widgets["templateWindowSize_denoising"].delete(0, tk.END)
            self.parameter_widgets["searchWindowSize_denoising"].delete(0, tk.END)

            self.parameter_widgets["h_denoising"].insert(0, str(self.h_val))
            self.parameter_widgets["hForColor_denoising"].insert(0, str(self.hForColor_val))
            self.parameter_widgets["templateWindowSize_denoising"].insert(0, str(self.templateWindowSize_val))
            self.parameter_widgets["searchWindowSize_denoising"].insert(0, str(self.searchWindowSize_val))

        if state != "NEW" and selected_filter == "Anisotropic Diffusion":
            self.num_iterations_val = int(self.parameter_widgets["num_iterations_diffusion"].get())
            self.kappa_val = float(self.parameter_widgets["kappa_diffusion"].get())
            self.gamma_val = float(self.parameter_widgets["gamma_diffusion"].get())
            self.option_val = int(self.parameter_widgets["option_diffusion"].get())

            # Define filter parameters as a dictionary
```

```python
        self.filter_params = {
            "num_iterations": self.num_iterations_val,
            "kappa": self.kappa_val,
            "gamma": self.gamma_val,
            "option": self.option_val
        }

        # Update filter params in the GUI
        self.parameter_widgets["num_iterations_diffusion"].delete(0, tk.END)
        self.parameter_widgets["kappa_diffusion"].delete(0, tk.END)
        self.parameter_widgets["gamma_diffusion"].delete(0, tk.END)
        self.parameter_widgets["option_diffusion"].delete(0, tk.END)

        self.parameter_widgets["num_iterations_diffusion"].insert(0, str(self.num_iterations_val))
        self.parameter_widgets["kappa_diffusion"].insert(0, str(self.kappa_val))
        self.parameter_widgets["gamma_diffusion"].insert(0, str(self.gamma_val))
        self.parameter_widgets["option_diffusion"].insert(0, str(self.option_val))

    if state != "NEW" and selected_filter == "Total Variation Denoising":
        self.weight_val = float(self.parameter_widgets["weight_denoising"].get())
        self.iterations_val = int(self.parameter_widgets["iterations_denoising"].get())

        # Define filter parameters as a dictionary
        self.filter_params = {
            "weight": self.weight_val,
            "iterations": self.iterations_val
        }

        # Update filter params in the GUI
        self.parameter_widgets["weight_denoising"].delete(0, tk.END)
        self.parameter_widgets["iterations_denoising"].delete(0, tk.END)

        self.parameter_widgets["weight_denoising"].insert(0, str(self.weight_val))
        self.parameter_widgets["iterations_denoising"].insert(0, str(self.iterations_val))

    if state != "NEW" and selected_filter == "Haar Wavelet Transform":
        self.wavelet_val = self.parameter_widgets["wavelet_type"].get()
        self.level_val = int(self.parameter_widgets["wavelet_level"].get())

        # Define filter parameters as a dictionary
        self.filter_params = {
            "wavelet": self.wavelet_val,
            "level": self.level_val
        }

        # Update filter params in the GUI
        self.parameter_widgets["wavelet_type"].delete(0, tk.END)
        self.parameter_widgets["wavelet_level"].delete(0, tk.END)

        self.parameter_widgets["wavelet_type"].insert(0, str(self.wavelet_val))
        self.parameter_widgets["wavelet_level"].insert(0, str(self.level_val))

    if state != "NEW" and selected_filter == "Haar Wavelet Transform":
```

```python
        self.wavelet_val = self.parameter_widgets["wavelet_type"].get()
        self.level_val = int(self.parameter_widgets["wavelet_level"].get())
        self.threshold_val = float(self.parameter_widgets["threshold"].get())

        # Define filter parameters as a dictionary
        self.filter_params = {
            "wavelet": self.wavelet_val,
            "level": self.level_val,
            "threshold": self.threshold_val
        }

        # Update filter params in the GUI
        self.parameter_widgets["wavelet_type"].delete(0, tk.END)
        self.parameter_widgets["wavelet_level"].delete(0, tk.END)
        self.parameter_widgets["threshold"].delete(0, tk.END)

        self.parameter_widgets["wavelet_type"].insert(0, str(self.wavelet_val))
        self.parameter_widgets["wavelet_level"].insert(0, str(self.level_val))
        self.parameter_widgets["threshold"].insert(0, str(self.threshold_val))

    if state != "NEW" and selected_filter == "Adaptive Thresholding":
        self.block_size_val = int(self.parameter_widgets["block_size"].get())
        self.c_val = int(self.parameter_widgets["c"].get())
        self.adaptive_method_val = self.parameter_widgets["adaptive_method"].get()
        self.threshold_type_val = self.parameter_widgets["threshold_type"].get()

        # Map adaptive method string value to integer value
        adaptive_methods           =           {"cv2.ADAPTIVE_THRESH_MEAN_C":
cv2.ADAPTIVE_THRESH_MEAN_C,
                          "cv2.ADAPTIVE_THRESH_GAUSSIAN_C":
cv2.ADAPTIVE_THRESH_GAUSSIAN_C}
        self.adaptive_method_val = adaptive_methods.get(self.adaptive_method_val)

        # Map threshold type string value to integer value
        threshold_types = {"cv2.THRESH_BINARY": cv2.THRESH_BINARY,
                          "cv2.THRESH_BINARY_INV": cv2.THRESH_BINARY_INV}
        self.threshold_type_val = threshold_types.get(self.threshold_type_val)

        # Define filter parameters as a dictionary
        self.filter_params = {
           "block_size": self.block_size_val,
           "C": self.c_val,
           "adaptive_method": self.adaptive_method_val,
           "threshold_type": self.threshold_type_val
        }

        # Update filter params in the GUI
        self.parameter_widgets["block_size"].delete(0, tk.END)
        self.parameter_widgets["c"].delete(0, tk.END)
        # Use set method with the correct syntax
self.parameter_widgets["adaptive_method"].set(str(self.adaptive_method_val))

self.parameter_widgets["threshold_type"].set(str(self.threshold_type_val))

        self.parameter_widgets["block_size"].insert(0, str(self.block_size_val))
        self.parameter_widgets["c"].insert(0, str(self.c_val))
```

```python
        if state != "NEW" and selected_filter == "Wiener Filter":
            self.kernel_size_val = int(self.parameter_widgets["kernel_size"].get())
            self.noise_var_val = float(self.parameter_widgets["noise_var"].get())

            # Define filter parameters as a dictionary
            self.filter_params = {
                "kernel_size": self.kernel_size_val,
                "noise_var": self.noise_var_val
            }

            # Update filter params in the GUI
            self.parameter_widgets["kernel_size"].delete(0, tk.END)
            self.parameter_widgets["noise_var"].delete(0, tk.END)

            self.parameter_widgets["kernel_size"].insert(0, str(self.kernel_size_val))
            self.parameter_widgets["noise_var"].insert(0, str(self.noise_var_val))

        return selected_filter

    def get_bilateral_params(self, filter_params):
        if "d_bilateral" in filter_params:
            d = filter_params["d_bilateral"]
        else:
            # default value
            d = 9

        if "sigma_color_bilateral" in filter_params:
            color = filter_params["sigma_color_bilateral"]
        else:
            # default value
            color = 75

        if "sigma_space_bilateral" in filter_params:
            space = filter_params["sigma_space_bilateral"]
        else:
            # default value
            space = 75

        return d, color, space

    def get_gaussian_params(self, filter_params):
        if "kernel_size_gaussian" in filter_params:
            kernel_size = filter_params["kernel_size_gaussian"]
        else:
            # default value
            kernel_size = 5

        if "sigma_gaussian" in filter_params:
            sigma = filter_params["sigma_gaussian"]
        else:
            # default value
            sigma = 0.1

        return kernel_size, sigma

    def get_median_params(self, filter_params):
        if "kernel_size_median" in filter_params:
```

```python
            kernel_size = filter_params["kernel_size_median"]
        else:
            # default value
            kernel_size = 5
        return kernel_size

    def get_mean_params(self, filter_params):
        if "kernel_size_mean" in filter_params:
            kernel_size = filter_params["kernel_size_mean"]
        else:
            # default value
            kernel_size = 5
        return kernel_size

    def get_nlm_denoising_params(self, filter_params):
        h = filter_params.get("h", 10)  # default value 10
        hForColor = filter_params.get("hForColor", 10)  # default value 10
        templateWindowSize = filter_params.get("templateWindowSize", 7)  # default value 7
        searchWindowSize = filter_params.get("searchWindowSize", 21)  # default value 21
        return h, hForColor, templateWindowSize, searchWindowSize

    def get_diffusion_params(self, filter_params):
        num_iterations = filter_params.get("num_iterations", 10)  # default value 10
        kappa = filter_params.get("kappa", 15)  # default value 15
        gamma = filter_params.get("gamma", 0.2)  # default value 0.2
        option = filter_params.get("option", 1)  # default value 1
        return num_iterations, kappa, gamma, option

    def get_total_variation_params(self, filter_params):
        weight = filter_params.get("weight", 0.01)  # default value 0.01
        iterations = filter_params.get("iterations", 20)  # default value 20
        return weight, iterations

    def get_haar_wavelet_params(self, filter_params):
        wavelet = filter_params.get("wavelet", "haar")  # default value "haar"
        level = filter_params.get("level", 1)  # default value 1
        threshold = filter_params.get("threshold", 0.0)  # default value 0.0
        return wavelet, level, threshold

    def get_adaptive_thresholding_params(self, filter_params):
        block_size = filter_params.get("block_size", 11)  # default value 11
        C = filter_params.get("C", 2)  # default value 2
        adaptive_method = filter_params.get("adaptive_method", cv2.ADAPTIVE_THRESH_MEAN_C)  # default value cv2.ADAPTIVE_THRESH_MEAN_C
        threshold_type = filter_params.get("threshold_type", cv2.THRESH_BINARY)  # default value cv2.THRESH_BINARY
        return block_size, C, adaptive_method, threshold_type

    def get_wiener_filter_params(self, filter_params):
        kernel_size = filter_params.get("kernel_size", 5)  # default value 5
        noise_var = filter_params.get("noise_var", 0.01)  # default value 0.01
        return kernel_size, noise_var

    def wiener_filter(self, frame, kernel_size=5, noise_var=0.01):
        # Check if frame is None
        if frame is None:
```

```python
        print("Error: Input frame is None.")
        return None

    # Check if frame is a valid numpy array
    if not isinstance(frame, np.ndarray):
        print("Error: Input frame is not a numpy array.")
        return None

    # Check if frame is an empty array
    if frame.size == 0:
        print("Error: Input frame is empty.")
        return None

    # Check if frame is in BGR color space
    if frame.shape[-1] != 3:
        print("Error: Input frame is not in BGR color space.")
        return None

    # Apply Wiener filter
    filtered_frame = cv2.medianBlur(frame, kernel_size)  # Use kernel_size[0] as the kernel size
    filtered_frame = cv2.fastNlMeansDenoising(filtered_frame, h=noise_var)
    return filtered_frame

def adaptive_threshold_each_channel(self, frame, block_size, C, adaptive_method, threshold_type):
    # Split the frame into individual channels
    b, g, r = cv2.split(frame)

    # Apply adaptive thresholding to each channel separately
    b_thresh = cv2.adaptiveThreshold(b, 255, adaptive_method, threshold_type, block_size, C)
    g_thresh = cv2.adaptiveThreshold(g, 255, adaptive_method, threshold_type, block_size, C)
    r_thresh = cv2.adaptiveThreshold(r, 255, adaptive_method, threshold_type, block_size, C)

    # Merge the thresholded channels back together
    return cv2.merge([b_thresh, g_thresh, r_thresh])


def haar_wavelet_transform(self, frame, wavelet='haar', level=1, threshold=0.1):
    def threshold_coeffs(coeffs, threshold):
        cA, (cH, cV, cD) = coeffs
        cH = pywt.threshold(cH, threshold, mode='soft')
        cV = pywt.threshold(cV, threshold, mode='soft')
        cD = pywt.threshold(cD, threshold, mode='soft')
        return cA, (cH, cV, cD)

    # Split the frame into its individual color channels
    b, g, r = cv2.split(frame)

    # Perform the wavelet transform and thresholding on each channel separately
    b_coeffs = pywt.wavedec2(b, wavelet, level=level)
    g_coeffs = pywt.wavedec2(g, wavelet, level=level)
    r_coeffs = pywt.wavedec2(r, wavelet, level=level)

    # Apply thresholding to the detail coefficients
```

```python
        b_coeffs = threshold_coeffs(b_coeffs, threshold)
        g_coeffs = threshold_coeffs(g_coeffs, threshold)
        r_coeffs = threshold_coeffs(r_coeffs, threshold)

        # Reconstruct the channels from the coefficients
        b_reconstructed = pywt.waverec2(b_coeffs, wavelet)
        g_reconstructed = pywt.waverec2(g_coeffs, wavelet)
        r_reconstructed = pywt.waverec2(r_coeffs, wavelet)

        # Clip the values to ensure they are within the valid range
        b_reconstructed = np.clip(b_reconstructed, 0, 255).astype(np.uint8)
        g_reconstructed = np.clip(g_reconstructed, 0, 255).astype(np.uint8)
        r_reconstructed = np.clip(r_reconstructed, 0, 255).astype(np.uint8)

        # Merge the channels back together
        return cv2.merge([b_reconstructed, g_reconstructed, r_reconstructed])

    def daubechies_wavelet_transform(self, frame):
        # Split the frame into its individual color channels
        b, g, r = cv2.split(frame)

        # Choose the wavelet function (Daubechies 5)
        wavelet = 'db5'

        # Perform the wavelet transform on each channel separately
        b_coeffs = pywt.dwt2(b, wavelet)
        g_coeffs = pywt.dwt2(g, wavelet)
        r_coeffs = pywt.dwt2(r, wavelet)

        # Reconstruct the channels from the coefficients
        b_reconstructed = pywt.idwt2(b_coeffs, wavelet)
        g_reconstructed = pywt.idwt2(g_coeffs, wavelet)
        r_reconstructed = pywt.idwt2(r_coeffs, wavelet)

        # Clip the values to ensure they are within the valid range
        b_reconstructed = np.clip(b_reconstructed, 0, 255).astype(np.uint8)
        g_reconstructed = np.clip(g_reconstructed, 0, 255).astype(np.uint8)
        r_reconstructed = np.clip(r_reconstructed, 0, 255).astype(np.uint8)

        # Merge the channels back together
        return cv2.merge([b_reconstructed, g_reconstructed, r_reconstructed])

    def anisotropic_diffusion(self, img, num_iterations=10, kappa=15, gamma=0.2, option=1):
        img = img.astype(np.float32)
        for i in range(num_iterations):
            # Compute gradients
            gradient_north = np.roll(img, -1, axis=0) - img
            gradient_south = np.roll(img, 1, axis=0) - img
            gradient_east = np.roll(img, -1, axis=1) - img
            gradient_west = np.roll(img, 1, axis=1) - img

            # Compute the diffusion coefficients based on gradient magnitude
            if option == 1:
                c_north = np.exp(-(gradient_north / kappa) ** 2)
                c_south = np.exp(-(gradient_south / kappa) ** 2)
                c_east = np.exp(-(gradient_east / kappa) ** 2)
                c_west = np.exp(-(gradient_west / kappa) ** 2)
```

```python
            elif option == 2:
                c_north = 1 / (1 + (gradient_north / kappa) ** 2)
                c_south = 1 / (1 + (gradient_south / kappa) ** 2)
                c_east = 1 / (1 + (gradient_east / kappa) ** 2)
                c_west = 1 / (1 + (gradient_west / kappa) ** 2)

            # Update image
            img += gamma * (c_north * gradient_north + c_south * gradient_south + c_east * gradient_east + c_west * gradient_west)

        return img.astype(np.uint8)

    def apply_total_variation_denoising_channel(self, channel, weight, iterations):
        # Initialize the result with the original channel
        result = channel.copy().astype(np.float64)  # Convert to float64

        # Perform total variation denoising
        for _ in range(iterations):
            # Compute the gradient of the channel
            dx = cv2.Sobel(result, cv2.CV_64F, 1, 0, ksize=3)
            dy = cv2.Sobel(result, cv2.CV_64F, 0, 1, ksize=3)

            # Update the channel using the gradient and the weight
            result -= weight * np.sqrt(dx**2 + dy**2)

        # Clip the values to ensure they are within the valid range
        result = np.clip(result, 0, 255).astype(np.uint8)

        return result

    def total_variation_denoising(self, img, weight=0.01, iterations=20):
        # Split the image into its individual color channels
        b, g, r = cv2.split(img)

        # Apply total variation denoising to each channel separately
        b_denoised = self.apply_total_variation_denoising_channel(b, weight, iterations)
        g_denoised = self.apply_total_variation_denoising_channel(g, weight, iterations)
        r_denoised = self.apply_total_variation_denoising_channel(r, weight, iterations)

        # Merge the denoised channels back together
        return cv2.merge([b_denoised, g_denoised, r_denoised])

    def apply_filter(self, filter_name, frame, filter_params=None):
        if filter_params is None:
            filter_params = {}
        if filter_name == "None":
            return frame
        elif filter_name == "Gaussian":
            kernel_size, sigma = self.get_gaussian_params(filter_params)
            return cv2.GaussianBlur(frame, (kernel_size,kernel_size), sigma)
        elif filter_name == "Mean":
            kernel_size = self.get_mean_params(filter_params)
            return cv2.blur(frame, (kernel_size, kernel_size))
        elif filter_name == "Median":
            kernel_size = self.get_median_params(filter_params)
```

```python
            return cv2.medianBlur(frame, kernel_size)
        elif filter_name == "Bilateral Filtering":
            d, color, space = self.get_bilateral_params(filter_params)
            return cv2.bilateralFilter(frame, d, color, space)
        elif filter_name == "Non-local Means Denoising":
            h, hForColor, templateWindowSize, searchWindowSize = self.get_nlm_denoising_params(filter_params)
            return cv2.fastNlMeansDenoisingColored(frame, None, h, hForColor, templateWindowSize, searchWindowSize)
        elif filter_name == "Anisotropic Diffusion":
            num_iterations, kappa, gamma, option = self.get_diffusion_params(filter_params)
            return self.anisotropic_diffusion(frame, num_iterations, kappa, gamma, option)
        elif filter_name == "Total Variation Denoising":
            weight, iterations = self.get_total_variation_params(filter_params)
            return self.total_variation_denoising(frame, weight, iterations)
        elif filter_name == "Wiener Filter":
            kernel_size, noise_var = self.get_wiener_filter_params(filter_params)
            print(kernel_size, noise_var)
            return self.wiener_filter(frame, kernel_size, noise_var)
        elif filter_name == "Adaptive Thresholding":
            block_size, C, adaptive_method, threshold_type = self.get_adaptive_thresholding_params(filter_params)
            return self.adaptive_threshold_each_channel(frame, block_size, C, adaptive_method, threshold_type)
        elif filter_name == "Haar Wavelet Transform":
            wavelet, level, threshold = self.get_haar_wavelet_params(filter_params)
            return self.haar_wavelet_transform(frame, wavelet, level, threshold)
        elif filter_name == "Daubechies Wavelet Transform":
            return self.daubechies_wavelet_transform(frame)
        else:
            return frame  # Default: return original frame if filter not foun

    def create_popup_window(self, cropped_fram, filter_name):
        self.popup_window = tk.Toplevel(self.master)
        self.popup_window.title(filter_name + " --- Cropped Image and Its Histogram")
        self.popup_window.geometry("1500x700")

        # Create a dictionary to store filter parameter widgets
        self.parameter_widgets = {}

        if filter_name == "Gaussian":
            frame = tk.Frame(self.popup_window)
            frame.pack()

            label_kernel = tk.Label(frame, text="Kernel Size:")
            label_kernel.pack(side="left")
            self.kernel_gaussian = tk.Entry(frame)
            self.kernel_gaussian.insert(0, "5")  # Default value
            self.kernel_gaussian.pack(side="left")
            self.parameter_widgets["kernel_size_gaussian"] = self.kernel_gaussian

            label_sigma = tk.Label(frame, text="Sigma:")
            label_sigma.pack(side="left")
            self.sigma_gaussian = tk.Entry(frame)
            self.sigma_gaussian.insert(0, "1.0")  # Default value
            self.sigma_gaussian.pack(side="left")
```

```
            self.parameter_widgets["sigma_gaussian"] = self.sigma_gaussian

        elif filter_name == "Median":
            tk.Label(self.popup_window, text="Kernel Size:").pack()
            self.kernel_median= tk.Entry(self.popup_window)
            self.kernel_median.insert(0, "5")  # Default value
            self.kernel_median.pack()
            self.parameter_widgets["kernel_size_median"] = self.kernel_median

        elif filter_name == "Mean":
            tk.Label(self.popup_window, text="Kernel Size:").pack()
            self.kernel_mean= tk.Entry(self.popup_window)
            self.kernel_mean.insert(0, "5")  # Default value
            self.kernel_mean.pack()
            self.parameter_widgets["kernel_size_mean"] = self.kernel_mean

        elif filter_name == "Bilateral Filtering":
            frame = tk.Frame(self.popup_window)
            frame.pack()

            label_d = tk.Label(frame, text="D:")
            label_d.pack(side="left")
            self.d_bilateral = tk.Entry(frame)
            self.d_bilateral.insert(0, "9")  # Default value
            self.d_bilateral.pack(side="left")
            self.parameter_widgets["d_bilateral"] = self.d_bilateral

            label_sigma_color = tk.Label(frame, text="Sigma Color:")
            label_sigma_color.pack(side="left")
            self.sigma_color_bilateral = tk.Entry(frame)
            self.sigma_color_bilateral.insert(0, "75.0")  # Default value
            self.sigma_color_bilateral.pack(side="left")
            self.parameter_widgets["sigma_color_bilateral"] = 
self.sigma_color_bilateral

            label_sigma_space = tk.Label(frame, text="Sigma Space:")
            label_sigma_space.pack(side="left")
            self.sigma_space_bilateral = tk.Entry(frame)
            self.sigma_space_bilateral.insert(0, "75.0")  # Default value
            self.sigma_space_bilateral.pack(side="left")
            self.parameter_widgets["sigma_space_bilateral"] = 
self.sigma_space_bilateral

        if filter_name == "Non-local Means Denoising":
            frame = tk.Frame(self.popup_window)
            frame.pack()

            label_h = tk.Label(frame, text="H:")
            label_h.pack(side="left")
            self.h_denoising = tk.Entry(frame)
            self.h_denoising.insert(0, "10")  # Default value
            self.h_denoising.pack(side="left")
            self.parameter_widgets["h_denoising"] = self.h_denoising

            label_hForColor = tk.Label(frame, text="HForColor:")
            label_hForColor.pack(side="left")
            self.hForColor_denoising = tk.Entry(frame)
            self.hForColor_denoising.insert(0, "10")  # Default value
```

```
            self.hForColor_denoising.pack(side="left")
            self.parameter_widgets["hForColor_denoising"] = self.hForColor_denoising

            label_templateWindowSize = tk.Label(frame, text="Template Window Size:")
            label_templateWindowSize.pack(side="left")
            self.templateWindowSize_denoising = tk.Entry(frame)
            self.templateWindowSize_denoising.insert(0, "7")  # Default value
            self.templateWindowSize_denoising.pack(side="left")
            self.parameter_widgets["templateWindowSize_denoising"] =
self.templateWindowSize_denoising

            label_searchWindowSize = tk.Label(frame, text="Search Window Size:")
            label_searchWindowSize.pack(side="left")
            self.searchWindowSize_denoising = tk.Entry(frame)
            self.searchWindowSize_denoising.insert(0, "21")  # Default value
            self.searchWindowSize_denoising.pack(side="left")
            self.parameter_widgets["searchWindowSize_denoising"] =
self.searchWindowSize_denoising

        if filter_name == "Anisotropic Diffusion":
            frame = tk.Frame(self.popup_window)
            frame.pack()

            label_num_iterations = tk.Label(frame, text="Number of Iterations:")
            label_num_iterations.pack(side="left")
            self.num_iterations_diffusion = tk.Entry(frame)
            self.num_iterations_diffusion.insert(0, "10")  # Default value
            self.num_iterations_diffusion.pack(side="left")
            self.parameter_widgets["num_iterations_diffusion"] =
self.num_iterations_diffusion

            label_kappa = tk.Label(frame, text="Kappa:")
            label_kappa.pack(side="left")
            self.kappa_diffusion = tk.Entry(frame)
            self.kappa_diffusion.insert(0, "15")  # Default value
            self.kappa_diffusion.pack(side="left")
            self.parameter_widgets["kappa_diffusion"] = self.kappa_diffusion

            label_gamma = tk.Label(frame, text="Gamma:")
            label_gamma.pack(side="left")
            self.gamma_diffusion = tk.Entry(frame)
            self.gamma_diffusion.insert(0, "0.2")  # Default value
            self.gamma_diffusion.pack(side="left")
            self.parameter_widgets["gamma_diffusion"] = self.gamma_diffusion

            label_option = tk.Label(frame, text="Option:")
            label_option.pack(side="left")
            self.option_diffusion = tk.Entry(frame)
            self.option_diffusion.insert(0, "1")  # Default value
            self.option_diffusion.pack(side="left")
            self.parameter_widgets["option_diffusion"] = self.option_diffusion

        if filter_name == "Total Variation Denoising":
            frame = tk.Frame(self.popup_window)
            frame.pack()

            label_weight = tk.Label(frame, text="Weight:")
            label_weight.pack(side="left")
```

```python
        self.weight_denoising = tk.Entry(frame)
        self.weight_denoising.insert(0, "0.01")  # Default value
        self.weight_denoising.pack(side="left")
        self.parameter_widgets["weight_denoising"] = self.weight_denoising

        label_iterations = tk.Label(frame, text="Iterations:")
        label_iterations.pack(side="left")
        self.iterations_denoising = tk.Entry(frame)
        self.iterations_denoising.insert(0, "20")  # Default value
        self.iterations_denoising.pack(side="left")
        self.parameter_widgets["iterations_denoising"] = self.iterations_denoising

    if filter_name == "Haar Wavelet Transform":
        frame = tk.Frame(self.popup_window)
        frame.pack()

        label_wavelet = tk.Label(frame, text="Wavelet Type:")
        label_wavelet.pack(side="left")
        self.wavelet_type = tk.Entry(frame)
        self.wavelet_type.insert(0, "haar")  # Default value
        self.wavelet_type.pack(side="left")
        self.parameter_widgets["wavelet_type"] = self.wavelet_type

        label_level = tk.Label(frame, text="Decomposition Level:")
        label_level.pack(side="left")
        self.wavelet_level = tk.Entry(frame)
        self.wavelet_level.insert(0, "1")  # Default value
        self.wavelet_level.pack(side="left")
        self.parameter_widgets["wavelet_level"] = self.wavelet_level

        label_threshold = tk.Label(frame, text="Threshold:")
        label_threshold.pack(side="left")
        self.threshold = tk.Entry(frame)
        self.threshold.insert(0, "0.1")  # Default value
        self.threshold.pack(side="left")
        self.parameter_widgets["threshold"] = self.threshold

    if filter_name == "Adaptive Thresholding":
        frame = tk.Frame(self.popup_window)
        frame.pack()

        label_block_size = tk.Label(frame, text="Block Size:")
        label_block_size.pack(side="left")
        self.block_size_entry = tk.Entry(frame)
        self.block_size_entry.insert(0, "11")  # Default value
        self.block_size_entry.pack(side="left")
        self.parameter_widgets["block_size"] = self.block_size_entry

        label_c = tk.Label(frame, text="C:")
        label_c.pack(side="left")
        self.c_entry = tk.Entry(frame)
        self.c_entry.insert(0, "2")  # Default value
        self.c_entry.pack(side="left")
        self.parameter_widgets["c"] = self.c_entry

        label_adaptive_method = tk.Label(frame, text="Adaptive Method:")
        label_adaptive_method.pack(side="left")
```

```python
        self.adaptive_method_entry                    =             ttk.Combobox(frame, 
values=[cv2.ADAPTIVE_THRESH_MEAN_C, cv2.ADAPTIVE_THRESH_GAUSSIAN_C])
        self.adaptive_method_entry.insert(0,  cv2.ADAPTIVE_THRESH_MEAN_C)        # 
Default value
        self.adaptive_method_entry.pack(side="left")
        self.parameter_widgets["adaptive_method"] = self.adaptive_method_entry

        label_threshold_type = tk.Label(frame, text="Threshold Type:")
        label_threshold_type.pack(side="left")
        self.threshold_type_entry = ttk.Combobox(frame, values=[cv2.THRESH_BINARY, 
cv2.THRESH_BINARY_INV])
        self.threshold_type_entry.insert(0, cv2.THRESH_BINARY)  # Default value
        self.threshold_type_entry.pack(side="left")
        self.parameter_widgets["threshold_type"] = self.threshold_type_entry

    if filter_name == "Wiener Filter":
        frame = tk.Frame(self.popup_window)
        frame.pack()

        label_kernel_size = tk.Label(frame, text="Kernel Size:")
        label_kernel_size.pack(side="left")
        self.kernel_size_entry = tk.Entry(frame)
        self.kernel_size_entry.insert(0, "5")  # Default value
        self.kernel_size_entry.pack(side="left")
        self.parameter_widgets["kernel_size"] = self.kernel_size_entry

        label_noise_var = tk.Label(frame, text="Noise Variance:")
        label_noise_var.pack(side="left")
        self.noise_var_entry = tk.Entry(frame)
        self.noise_var_entry.insert(0, "0.01")  # Default value
        self.noise_var_entry.pack(side="left")
        self.parameter_widgets["noise_var"] = self.noise_var_entry

    # Frame for Apply and Save buttons
    button_frame = tk.Frame(self.popup_window)
    button_frame.pack()

    # Add an Apply button to apply the filter
    apply_button        =        tk.Button(button_frame,            text="Apply", 
command=lambda:self.analyze_histogram("OLD"))
    apply_button.pack(side="left")

    # Add a Save button to save the filtered image
    save_button        =             tk.Button(button_frame,             text="Save", 
command=self.save_filtered_image)
    save_button.pack(side="left")

def save_filtered_image(self):
    # Ask the user for a location and filename to save the image
    file_path       =       filedialog.asksaveasfilename(defaultextension=".png", 
filetypes=[("PNG files", "*.png"), ("JPEG files", "*.jpg"), ("All files", "*.*")])

    if file_path and self.cropped_img is not None:
        # Ensure self.cropped_img is a valid numpy array and convert to RGB
        cropped_img_array = np.array(self.cropped_img)
        cropped_img_rgb = cv2.cvtColor(cropped_img_array, cv2.COLOR_BGR2RGB)
        cv2.imwrite(file_path, cropped_img_rgb)
```

```python
    def run_outside_script(self, file_name):
        try:
            # Get the absolute path of the external script
            script_directory = os.path.dirname(os.path.abspath(__file__))
            script_path = os.path.join(script_directory, file_name)

            # Print the path for debugging
            print(f"Absolute script path: {script_path}")

            if not os.path.exists(script_path):
                print(f"File {script_path} not found.")
                return

            # Call the external script using the absolute path
            process = subprocess.Popen(["python", script_path], shell=True)
            process.communicate()  # Wait for the process to finish
            print("Script executed successfully.")

        except Exception as e:
            print(f"An error occurred while running the script: {e}")

    def choose_matcher(self):
        selected_matcher = self.matcher_combobox.get()
        if selected_matcher == "SIFT":
            self.run_outside_script("SIFTMacher_NEW.py")
        elif selected_matcher == "ORB":
            self.run_outside_script("ORBMacher.py")
        elif selected_matcher == "FAST":
            self.run_outside_script("FASTMatcher.py")
        elif selected_matcher == "AGAST":
            self.run_outside_script("AGASTMatcher.py")
        elif selected_matcher == "BRISK":
            self.run_outside_script("BRISKMatcher.py")
        elif selected_matcher == "AKAZE":
            self.run_outside_script("AKAZEMatcher.py")

    def open_new_instance(self):
        # Open another instance of the application
        root = tk.Toplevel(self.master)
        app = Filter_CroppedFrame(root)

def main():
    root = tk.Tk()
    app = Filter_CroppedFrame(root)
    root.mainloop()

if __name__ == "__main__":
    main()
```

Bibliography

Vivian Siahaan and Rismon Hasiholan Sianipar. *TKINTER, DATA SCIENCE, AND MACHINE LEARNING*. North Sumatera: Balige Publishing, 2023.

Vivian Siahaan and Rismon Hasiholan Sianipar. *DATA VISUALIZATION, TIME-SERIES FORECASTING, AND PREDICTION USING MACHINE LEARNING WITH TKINTER*. North Sumatera: Balige Publishing, 2023.

Vivian Siahaan and Rismon Hasiholan Sianipar. *TIME-SERIES WEATHER FORECASTING AND PREDICTION USING MACHINE LEARNING WITH TKINTER*. North Sumatera: Balige Publishing, 2023.

Vivian Siahaan and Rismon Hasiholan Sianipar. DATA VISUALIZATION, TIME-SERIES FORECASTING, AND PREDICTION USING MACHINE LEARNING WITH TKINTER. North Sumatera: Balige Publishing, 2023.

Vivian Siahaan and Rismon Hasiholan Sianipar. START FROM SCRATCH DIGITAL SIGNAL PROCESSING WITH TKINTER. North Sumatera: Balige Publishing, 2023.

Vivian Siahaan and Rismon Hasiholan Sianipar. START FROM SCRATCH DIGITAL IMAGE PROCESSING WITH TKINTER. North Sumatera: Balige Publishing, 2023.

Vivian Siahaan and Rismon Hasiholan Sianipar. START FROM SCRATCH DIGITAL IMAGE PROCESSING WITH TKINTER. North Sumatera: Balige Publishing, 2023.

Vivian Siahaan and Rismon Hasiholan Sianipar. IMAGE DENOISING, EDGE DETECTION, AND SEGMENTATION WITH TKINTER. North Sumatera: Balige Publishing, 2023.

Vivian Siahaan and Rismon Hasiholan Sianipar. DIGITAL VIDEO PROCESSING PROJECTS USING PYTHON AND TKINTER. North Sumatera: Balige Publishing, 2024.

Vivian Siahaan and Rismon Hasiholan Sianipar. FRAME ANALYSIS AND PROCESSING IN DIGITAL VIDEO USING PYTHON AND TKINTER. North Sumatera: Balige Publishing, 2024.

Vivian Siahaan and Rismon Hasiholan Sianipar. MOTION ANALYSIS AND OBJECT TRACKING USING PYTHON AND TKINTER. North Sumatera: Balige Publishing, 2024.

Vivian Siahaan and Rismon Hasiholan Sianipar. FRAME FILTERING AND EDGES-DETECTION USING PYTHON AND TKINTER. North Sumatera: Balige Publishing, 2024.

Vivian Siahaan and Rismon Hasiholan Sianipar. OPTICAL FLOW ANALYSIS AND MOTION ESTIMATION IN DIGITAL VIDEO WITH PYTHON AND TKINTER. North Sumatera: Balige Publishing, 2024.

Vivian Siahaan and Rismon Hasiholan Sianipar. GRADIENT-BASED BLOCK MATCHING MOTION ESTIMATION AND OBJECT TRACKING WITH PYTHON AND TKINTER. North Sumatera: Balige Publishing, 2024.

Vivian Siahaan and Rismon Hasiholan Sianipar. FEATURES-BASED MOTION ESTIMATION AND OBJECT TRACKING WITH PYTHON AND TKINTER. North Sumatera: Balige Publishing, 2024

www.ingramcontent.com/pod-product-compliance
Lightning Source LLC
Chambersburg PA
CBHW082108220526
45472CB00009B/2089